No Tir

Like the

Memories of the Good Old Days
in East Anglia

~

Jean Turner

COUNTRYSIDE BOOKS

NEWBURY, BERKSHIRE

First published 1997
© Jean Turner 1997
Reprinted 2000

COUNTRYSIDE BOOKS
3 Catherine Road
Newbury, Berkshire

To view our complete range of books,
please visit us at
www.countrysidebooks.co.uk

ISBN 1 853206 467 X

In memory of my dear mother.

Produced through MRM Associates Ltd., Reading
Printed by J. W. Arrowsmith Ltd., Bristol

Contents

———— ❧ ————

Foreword

————— ❧ —————

When I was asked to think about writing this book, I really needed no persuading. During the research for my book *East Anglian Privies* I had realised what a long, steady haul life has taken this century to get us where we are today. Twenty-four hour a day television, mobile telephones, dishwashers and all the other paraphernalia of a materialistic age – but have we really benefited? Children can no longer play safely away from home, loneliness is a problem, crime has soared. Nobody will disagree when I say that though life was hard earlier this century, somewhere along the road to progress we have lost something valuable.

East Anglian folk are my special interest; not surprisingly, because I was raised in the Norfolk countryside, amongst the agricultural fraternity. The Norfolk dialect is music to my ears and I particularly admire the humour, honesty and down-to-earth approach of country people who have lived their lives close to the soil. The real life stories in this book will lead the reader to his or her own conclusions. Certainly, the world must move on and we would want it no other way, but certain values and standards that were once a part of everyday life could well carry us forward on a more cheerful and positive note. It is not too late to look to the past for valuable advice.

I have enjoyed researching this book; talking to and corresponding with lots of East Anglian people. Happy memories make for great clarity of remembrance and I am indebted to all who wrote to me. I am sorry I could not use all the material. I would particularly like to thank those who sent in old photographs; and special thanks

to Mr Phil Colman of Old Catton who always comes to my rescue.

I do hope you enjoy these stories – humorous, sad and instructive – and that they will help you recapture some of the good times we all used to have.

Jean Turner

Tin Bath Night

———— ❧ ————

'I have very fond memories of our bath nights in front of the roaring kitchen fire when the crackle and whisper of the grate would lull one into a relaxed state of mind and mother's amicable countenance presided. More often than not the radio would be playing and we always ended up having something delicious to eat with a cup of hot chocolate.'

M y father was a herdsman all his working life, up at the crack of dawn to milk cows ('best part of the day'). Mother looked after the home, Father and we three girls. As we approached our teens Mother spent time fruit picking and doing other seasonal work on local farms. Born and bred in Norwich, Mother loved her outdoor employment. Mum and Dad had always been used to the tin bath ritual once a week and no one was more socially upgraded than I when we moved from Heckingham to Hales, a distance of approximately one and a half miles, to be nearer school. This sort of move was very familiar to my mother. Father often changed houses without actually changing employer. A kind of cleansing process whereby we dumped all accumulated rubbish and started excitingly afresh without losing friends.

We moved to Hales and a bathroom all right, but there the convenience and comfort ended. The new bathroom only had a cold water tap. Mother still had to heat the water, albeit in a brand new Burco boiler, and carry it into the bathroom. Whatever grand ideas above my station I nurtured were quickly squashed because we were still only allowed to bath once a week.

The new bathroom was not all it pretended to be; unheated, it was as cold as charity. At least the old galvanised tin bath we had previously used had always been triumphantly placed in front of a roaring hot open fire. More importantly, I missed the jovial atmosphere of bathing with my two sisters. No more teasing, no more watching each other giggle as Mother washed and tickled. The only thing going for the new bathroom was privacy; very much appreciated because I was developing and getting quite nervy on tin bath nights in case anybody should call. The last person I wanted to educate was a late grocery roundsman. My little bits and pieces were not for show.

Although we had progressed to a bathroom, we were still ungraced on the domestic front in that we had to use an outside loo – a cute little semi-detached building a long way down the garden path. An area of endurance I had hoped to see the back of. But the new bathroom elegance did extend to an improved service in the sanitation stakes – a static chamberpot. So convenient when one wanted to go whilst in the bath. I had suspected that for years my sister Jennifer, the scamp that she was, had delicately trickled in the tin bath despite Mother's cries of 'anybody want to wee-wee' before entering.

Nevertheless, I have very fond memories of our bath nights in front of the roaring kitchen fire when the crackle and whisper of the grate would lull one into a relaxed state of mind and Mother's amicable countenance presided. When my sisters and I would gleefully sit around watching one another take their turn. We all felt wonderfully refreshed after this weekly treatment, the sort of intimate family get-together rarely experienced nowadays. I remember the pure luxury of warmed towels and underwear ready and waiting. Winceyette nighties were never more comfortable. More often than not the radio would be playing and we always ended up having something delicious to eat with a cup of hot chocolate.

Winter nights were great fun, especially if the wind happened to be whistling around the house; then it was almost an adventure to sit in the tin bath. From what I can remember, we all stayed up for as long as our eyes stayed open on bath nights. As this was always at the weekend it did not matter because there was no school the following day. For sure we needed no rocking on these nights.

David Broom of Gillingham remembers bath night at Hill Farm, Heckingham: 'Saturday night was bath night for us all and for the rest of the week we would have a strip wash before bed. Late on Saturday afternoon Father would fill the copper in the wash-house and light the fire in the grate underneath. The water would heat while we had tea. After tea Father would bring in the tin bath and place it in front of the cooking range in the farmhouse kitchen. He would bring one bucket of cold and three buckets of hot. Being the youngest I was first in; after a good wash of the hair

David Broom's sketch of bath night at Hill Farm, Heckingham.

Joy Calton and her younger sister Wendy. 'The bath was also used for soaking the sheets my grandmother laundered during the war for the local GIs.'

and body I was lifted out, dried and put to bed. Father would then go out and bring in one bucket of hot water to top up the bath before my sister got in to be washed from top to toe before also being put to bed. More topping up so that Mother could have her bath and then it was Father's turn. This event would take up the whole of Saturday evening. In winter months a good fire would be warming us, the old Tilley lamp would be illuminating the room and music would be coming from the old accumulator radio on top of the chest of drawers.

'Sunday morning and we would wake up to the sound of Father scooping up the water from the tin bath with a hand cup and taking it all back outside by the bucketful. To get the last of the water out, the bath would be stood on end. In summer the water would be thrown onto the vegetable garden. Once empty the bath would be hung back in the wash-house until the next Saturday. I had ten to twelve years' bathing in front of the fire. My sister, mum and dad a few more years than that. My wife who was born and brought up in Ruby Street, Leicester, can well remember the tin bath that hung outside on a party wall, like many more terraced houses in the city.'

Dr P. D. Rawlence of Pulham Market spent 30 years in general practice in rural south Norfolk, 1951 to 1981. 'When I started it was the rule to hold surgery on Saturday evenings. I protested about this as no other practice to my knowledge was retaining this service. Upon asking the then senior partner why, he replied, "Oh, it's bath night on Saturday and they like to come to the surgery clean and fresh." The tin bath was occasionally occupied at other times, as I found out a few times on entering a cottage and finding a large fat mum taking ablutions.'

'My two sisters and I were brought up before the Second World War in a one-room-downstairs labourer's cottage in the middle of nowhere,' remembers Canon Derek W. Price who now lives at Dereham, Norfolk. 'Saturday night was memorable for several things. *In Town Tonight* ("lovely sweet raspberries"), *Music Hall* or *Palace of Varieties* on the wireless with people like Gracie Fields and George Robey. But chiefly when we were very young, for the baths in front of the open blackleaded fire grate. The water was carried in buckets from a flowing stream in a nearby wood, or if it had been raining, from the outside butt. The latter water was preferred because it was soft. The water was heated in saucepans or kettles suspended over an open coal fire. The rug in front of the fire was hand-made from pieces of material. Of course, we all washed in the same water, which was afterwards poured down a drain outside or used to water the garden in dry weather. Mother, with an apron made from sacking, washed us thoroughly with red carbolic soap and then did our hair, rinsing it with a jug of tepid water. We were not allowed outside after hair washing in case of catching cold. When the bath ritual was finished we put on clean clothes which had been aired first under one of the bed mattresses and then on a clothes horse or chair-back before the fire. Fresh underwear was hung on a line underneath the mantelpiece ready for Sunday mornings.

'Some Saturday evenings we had a spoonful of syrup of figs to clean us out; the only good it did me was to prevent me from going to church the next morning! Occasionally Dad cycled to the local pub and if we waited up, he returned with a packet of Smith's crisps. Mum got a bottle of stout. After that it was up the winding stairs to bed with a candle. As we grew older, bathing with others around became impossible. We sometimes stood in the bath with underpants or knickers on and, as Mother used to say, "washed up as far us possible and down as far as possible". "Possible" had to be washed in private. Believe it or not the luxury of warm tap water was not enjoyed until about ten years ago. Though when it did arrive it did not make us any cleaner than when we had used saucepans and kettles.'

Mrs Janet Seaman of Lowestoft remembers outside bathing: 'My mother had six children. We lived at Walsham Hall, Mendham, a big cold farmhouse. During the winter months we had a large fire which burnt big logs of wood. Mother would place a wooden clothes horse around us draped with towels to keep out the draughts. During the summer we had our bath on the lawn which was great fun as we were able to splash about. How times change. Now children have a bath nearly every night in a lovely warm bathroom.'

Frank Viner remembers encounters with the copper: 'I do remember the long tin bath in front of the kitchener, also the hip bath with one's feet dangling out. But I particularly remember the copper. After clothes washing this was used to supplement the bath, but some water was left in the copper for my bath. I remember the rim of the copper being so much warmer than the water and the effect it had on my little bottom!'

What has stayed in Mrs P. Banham's mind is the baker's visit at bathtime. She now lives at Pakefield in Suffolk: 'I was about eight years old in the mid-1930s. I had two sisters and a brother all under the age of ten. We lived in a very old cottage with the front door opening onto the main road. Late every Saturday afternoon Mum and Dad would fill all the heavy black saucepans with water. They placed the tin bath, which would be hanging outside on the wall, in front of the fire. Then it would be make up your mind time because nobody wanted to undress when it was cold in winter.

'I think what stands out most in my mind was the winter. One of us would be in the bath when there would be a loud knock on the door. Mr Middleton, our baker, with his large basket hanging over his arm would be standing there. Always smiling, the door wide, while Mum paid him. There would be gusts of wind, sometimes snow, blowing in through the door and one of us shivering in the bath. But there was a happy ending – the baker always gave Mum a small currant loaf saying how the children would like that after their bath. And believe me, I can always remember those beautiful slices of currant bread after our bath.'

Mrs Hazel Derbyshire, now of Manningtree in Essex, has had trouble convincing her children that she did actually live like this! 'There were four daughters and one son in our family. We lived in a small terraced house and the stone copper was in the scullery. This was lit first thing on Monday morning and was going all day for the washing (always cold meat and pickles that day), then lit again on Fridays for our weekly bath and hair wash. In her young days my mother was a housemaid for Lord and Lady Astor, so she was very strict about everything; us and the home. When we all left home in the 1950s my father had a proper bath put in the kitchen covered by a wooden board. A gas geyser stood over it.

'I had a large family, six daughters, and we lived in a six-bedroomed house in Dovercourt with bathroom and two toilets. The children were always having baths. When I talk about my young life they just cannot imagine it! Winters seemed colder then, no central heating, cotton sheets – and we made patterns on the inside of windows in the winter when Jack Frost had been. We didn't have a cold from one year to the next!'

'At 64 years old I don't feel like a fossil but by many people's reckoning I must be!' said Mrs H. Durrell of Stratford St Andrew,

Suffolk. 'As a small child my earliest recollections are of the tin bath hanging on a nail in the wash-house. Memories are of the lovely warmth and attention that surrounded bath night. Everyone, it seemed, used to come and watch "baby being bathed". Interestingly enough, there was a normal bath in the house; I presume it had drainage and at least a cold water supply but I don't ever remember it being used. The real bath was actually in the kitchen and had a wooden cover which enabled it to be used as a dumping ground for all items going into and out of the kitchen. When I married and moved to a cottage without a bathroom our small tin bath hung outside the back door. We had a kitchen range and a gas boiler so there was water in abundance. As an adult it was less fun when the drying and dressing was followed by emptying and cleaning the bath. I only wish that on just one occasion I could have bathed in a hip bath in a bedroom – just think how grand that must have been!'

Mrs C. M. High of Thetford joined the Women's Land Army in 1943 and after training was sent to work on a mixed farm about eight miles from King's Lynn. 'There was no piped water or electricity, just a pump over the sink and oil lamps. On Friday nights after the farmer had gone to bed I was allowed a bath in a bungalow bath in front of the sitting room fire, watched by the farmer's daughter who kept house for him plus an evacuee lady who lived in the parlour with her three children. We all sat together in the evenings. Kettles were boiled on an open fire and cold water came from the pump. I found it all a bit embarrassing at first as I had been used to a proper bathroom and privacy at home, but I soon got used to it. Summer time I took the bath and water up to a spare room as the farmer stayed up much later, but it was quite a job carrying water up steep narrow stairs.'

Large families had special problems on bath night, as Mrs V. Percival of Ardleigh, Essex, remembers. 'At one time there were nine of us taking our turns although this number dropped to six during the war years. Looking back I don't know how we managed to all get bathed in one night. As children we went in two at a time. We had no lock on the door between the kitchen and living room but we always kept a towel at the ready just in case. Those in the living room would cry out, "So-and-so is in the bath" if anybody tried to enter. At Christmas time our bath was used to pluck the cockerels; they were killed and boiling water poured over them; that made the feathers easier to remove.'

G. J. Humphrey, now of Brantham in Essex, still cherishes memories of tin baths in front of the fire. 'Dad always came home early on Saturdays, 4 pm, and I would join him on his trip to the well shared by three other cottages. Here the menfolk gathered and talked as they drew up enough water for their family baths. By tea-time the fire was made up and a recharged accumulator fitted to the wireless. After tea the tin bath was placed in front of the fire. I was allowed into the bath after my hair had been washed over the kitchen sink. The wireless was switched on for *In Town Tonight* (a

Mrs C. M. High of Thetford, bathing her son on the kitchen table.

voice shouted STOP! and all the London traffic stopped). I was allowed to stay in the bath until the programme ended.

'Then, as a young fireman on a steam engine, one of our duties was to work a slow goods train from Norwich to Ipswich in the afternoon. Between Mellis and Finningham a very well-built lady crossing-keeper always took her bath in summer time under her apple tree. A whistle from the engine was always returned by a friendly wave. My driver would say, "Cleanliness is next to godliness".

'In the 1960s we moved into a railway cottage in Leyton, London, complete with outside loo and tin bath. A new experience for our sons but they soon learnt to enjoy bath nights. They would help me fill the bath, which was placed to the right of the gas fire. Being small they all jumped in together. My wife and I preferred to bath in the kitchen next to the gas oven – it was more convenient for emptying after. I would just open the back door and tip (a bit cold when in the altogether sometimes). The neighbours

Mr G. J. Humphrey's sons on bath night.

always went to bed early, except for one night I forgot their son and daughter were home on holiday. They were a bit surprised when I opened my back door, tipped out the bath water, said goodnight and closed the door! I still empty the tin bath each week but now it is used in the garden by three ducks and a drake.'

Mrs E. F. Bates of Great Waldringfield, Suffolk, remembers a curious case: 'When I worked for a London solicitor over 30 years ago, a man cited an incident with a tin bath as part of his divorce case. I guess it came under the heading of "cruelty" in those days. Apparently, whenever the man took his bath in front of the fire his wife used to regularly go and fry sausages on the fire!'

Mrs K. A. King now lives at Glemsford, Suffolk, but grew up in north London in the 1950s. 'Friday night was bath night for my two older brothers, Mum, Dad and me. Being the youngest, and luckiest, I always got in first so had clean water. Mum just removed the scum before the boys got in. I remember one summer when my brother had netted a fair-sized roach in the park pond. We usually put back all the tiddlers, sticklebacks and newts but since this was a good size it was brought home and put in the tin bath to swim. One or two rocks were placed in said bath along with some green pond weed. All very well until Friday night came when all this debris had to be removed. The roach was popped into the washing up bowl until Saturday morning.

'By the time I was eleven I was going to my friend's house and sharing her bath since it was much easier. Although in winter this was perishing cold as the family were poor and only had a tiny fire which was fed on orange boxes. I eventually joined my brothers and went to the public baths in Hackney. I believe a bath cost about sevenpence but one got a real deep bath full of lovely hot water – and privacy. Problem was one only had a certain amount of time before the attendant banged on the door. When I reached 14 we moved into an upstairs flat with bathroom, although we still had to heat the water. Dad soon had an Ascot water heater fitted so we had running hot water in the bathroom – such bliss! Haven't we come a long way since the tin bath days?'

Everyone lived this way, no matter where in the country you lived. P. W. Jones of Woolpit, Suffolk, was billeted in a miner's home in Yorkshire in the 1940s, along with two other young men, having been called up under the Bevan Scheme. 'The miner's home consisted of two bedrooms up and two rooms down, with a toilet at the bottom of the yard. The tin bath was hung from a hook on the outside wall. The only source of water was a cold tap and a small Ascot heater over the sink. The pit I was assigned to had no pit-head baths and operated a three-shift system. As we all had the same shift it meant we arrived home at 2.30 pm.

'Our landlady would have a meal ready and when we had eaten she would then leave the room whilst we proceeded with the daily chore of bathing. We brought in the tin bath, put it in front of the fire and filled it to a depth of approximately four inches with hot water from the Ascot. Because there were three of us daily, we had a rota, so that each person had a first bath every third day, which in practice meant that after the first man had washed all his pit dirt off, the next would put in more hot water and take his bath. When it came to the third person he was faced with pretty dirty water. But it was war time and had to be accepted. We then had to empty by using an old saucepan. Ironically, a year after I got demobbed in 1947, the pits, having been nationalised, were supplied with pit-head baths, so the ritual I've just described stopped.'

George E. Read was born at Cretingham, a small village in east Suffolk, 70 years ago. 'I was one of four children. Father was a horseman on a farm; we lived in a small cottage which went with the job. Our only water supply was the village pump – fortunately just across the road from us. Bathrooms were for the better-off members of society so the humble tin bath came into its own in more ways than one. On Monday morning for the weekly wash and on Saturday night for the bath. I shall never forget one Saturday night during the winter when this routine of bathing was in full swing. Having just finished bathing I was busy drying myself and to make things easier I put one foot on the edge of the bath. My older sister decided to pinch my bottom whereupon I transferred all my weight onto the edge of the bath and, yes, you've guessed, over went the bath – water everywhere.'

Of course, no occasion is complete without the odd funny story. Bath night in front of the fire was no exception, as these recollections have shown.

Apart from the unexpected caller most 'townie' visitors were visibly shaken by this show of apparent abandonment. When offered this chance of bodily cleanliness, they ran. One women told me, 'I had a rather posh city cousin staying one week. She was very sentimental about personal hygiene and her modesty was exasperating at times. You see, I was used to country ways and mischievous brothers. She was an only child and lived in a house with a bathroom.

'Now, when Friday evening came she was completely fascinated by our tin bath affair in front of the kitchen fire, *until* she was invited to take her turn. One on my brothers had taken a shine to her and I think she was scared stiff he might come prancing into the room whilst she was naked. She refused point blank. After a short verbal struggle with my mother, who assured her my brother was not in the vicinity, she got into the bath, and giggled from the moment she got in. It was only years later she told me that it was the nearest to paradise she had ever got!'

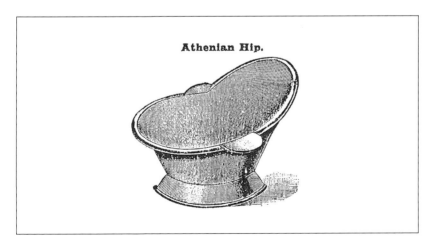

Athenian Hip.

Home Births

--- ❧ ---

'I'm sorry Doctor, I just stood up and out 'e come.'

At their annual Scarborough Conference a few years ago, the
Royal College of Midwives were told that delivery rooms in
hospitals were becoming like football terraces. 'Childbirth is
becoming a spectator sport.'

A far cry from yesteryear when most births took place in the
familiarity of one's own home; in the warmth and quiet of a well-
lit bedroom with perhaps an open fire for added comfort. When
the family all congregated in another room awaiting that familiar
first little cry. When over-nervous expectant fathers were sent to
the pub with, 'Git yew out o' the way; yew done enough damage
already!' And when that same father returned to proudly congrat-
ulate his wife, the moving experience would reduce him to tears.
'Take no notice of 'im,' the midwife would beam, 'it's the beer!',
satisfaction all over her face for yet another local baby safely delivered.

Home births were the norm. The family had probably been
paying into a nursing association scheme each week for just such
an expected event. A doctor was only ever called if the birth
became complicated or a stitch was required. On the whole, midwives coped admirably; some even cursing if somebody sent for a
doctor, which they felt undermined their authority.

Pregnancies were hush-hush in some circles early this century.
Some well-bred women actually hid themselves away until after

This was the bedroom, in the early 1900s, of solicitor's wife Mrs Tillett of Old Catton, near Norwich. Note the wonderful brass bed and the draped fireplace.

the event; or went so far as employing wet nannies after the birth – women who would breast-feed their baby, allowing the new mother to continue her social life without interruption. Polite enquires would receive the stony reply, 'Baby is doing fine; nanny is doing a wonderful job.'

Unlike working people, who treated childbirth as nothing except natural. Their down-to-earth sense of humour pulled no punches. 'Like layin' an egg worn't it, missus?' a cheerful neighbour might well joke, only to be verbally crushed with, 'Yew try havin' one. Then there'd be some squawking!'

It is interesting to note what the book, *The Universal Home Doctor*, had to say in 1935: 'BIRTH – If the child arrives after only seven months it is said to be premature. It may still live and in time become strong but will require very careful attention in its early years. A birth earlier than six months, and a half, but later than three months, is called a miscarriage. Before three months it is an abortion. The birth of all babies born after 28 weeks of pregnancy, whether alive or dead, must be notified to the Medical Office of Health at the district within 36 hours. This must be done by the father or any person in attendance on the mother at the time of birth. In addition the birth must be registered with the Registrar of Births, Marriages and Deaths. It is a criminal offence to conceal a birth.'

Let us, then, consider the real problems at the time. First, there were very few telephones in the home. Only the wealthy and doctors had such communications at their disposal. District nurses and midwives worked in a quite plain and simple way – although it has to be said it was a most practical way – and bumped along, as one gentlemen stated, 'like a rabbit flung into a poacher's bag'. Each morning the local midwife would leave her house to go on her rounds, but not before leaving a card in her window, giving details of names and addresses where she could be found that day. It was then necessary for, usually, the father to cycle round to each address until he found her. The midwife would, if not already involved in a labour, hop onto her own cycle and follow in hot pursuit.

Mrs B. Scopes of Ipswich was a midwife in the 1930s: 'Leiston & District (Suffolk) had a nursing association with a secretary. Anyone could pay into this; as far as I can remember it was about one old penny a week. Those who subscribed received general nursing free, those who did not paid two shillings a visit. Antenatal was free for expectant mothers. For actual confinement it was about £2 if they were members, but about £5 for non-members. I collected the money each month and gave it to the secretary. Regarding doctors' fees, I filled in three forms. One for the doctor, one for County Hall, and one for myself. I do not remember any charge for miscarriages. The ones I dealt with did not need a doctor.

'Sterilizing was done in the patient's own home. We used a square biscuit tin from the grocer. We rolled up pads, made cotton wool swabs and packed them into the tin and baked them in the oven. These were not opened till needed. I carried a midwifery bag on the back of my cycle with various instruments and dishes which I put in a saucepan and boiled in the home on arrival and again when I finished. I had to fill in records daily; I also had a register to enter calls (name of patient, treatment etc). This I took once a month to the secretary of the nursing association. If patients had any complaints they reported to her. (Glad to say I never had any.) Most homes had an old-fashioned wash-stand with bowl and jug. Babies were bathed in the bowl. In two cases I had, we used a drawer out of a tallboy for baby's cradle.'

How did the rest of the family cope with all this medical activity? Mrs E. Cullum of Spixworth near Norwich is almost 90 years of age. She remembers those days very well. 'For a start there were no doors locked and neighbours were friends who rallied round, helping with the washing. There were eight girls and four boys in our family, so we had plenty of visits from the midwife. At one of these times my eldest sister had the first week off school to help, the one younger than her had the second week off. We all had jobs to do. When I was eight my job was to look after three younger children. For all that my mother lived to be 93 and never went into hospital.'

Another lady, now well into her eighties, wrote: 'My grannie had a lot of babies. I was told about 20. All lived very long lives. I've often wondered how they managed – no electricity, just an oil lamp, water pump outside, a coal and wood fire to cook on. No disposable nappies then. Grandad had to travel six miles by horse and cart to summon the doctor at one event. It must have been very hard, but all, including my mother, lived a good, long and happy life.'

In those not-too-far-off days there was a real sense of community. Nobody felt burdened by helping others because one day their assistance would, more than likely, be returned. There was always a tough local woman who could be relied upon to help out in times of emergency. Such women were adaptable and could

A family photograph – four children very close in age.

turn their hand to any domestic problem. However, many were not trained, although probably quite experienced in delivering babies, and concerned families only contacted such women in real emergencies because the local midwife, naturally, did not take kindly to an inexperienced stranger emerging champion. Given half the chance, many midwives would have trampled them into the dust, but to be fair, such women were saints in times of crisis.

Everybody mucked in, as Mr Phil Colman of Old Catton, Norfolk recalls. 'It was April 9th, 1916. My mother sent the maid for Granny Rump who lived in a cottage near the blacksmith's shop. Granny Rump laid out the dead, made sausages for farmers when they killed their pigs, and was also the village midwife. As soon as she saw Mother she instructed Father to "get the doctor as quick as you can". Father saddled his horse and was away as fast as the horse could gallop. Due to the skill of Granny Rump and Doctor, I arrived that night. After the doctor had left, Granny Rump put a red hot cinder from the fireplace in a saucepan of water. When the water cooled, she put it in my bottle and gave it to me. Father asked what she was doing. She replied, "Now he has drunk this, he will grow to be a strong man and live a long life." Father was so pleased to have a son, he promised Granny Rump he would send her a Christmas dinner every year for the rest of her life. I took her last Christmas chicken dinner and pudding when I was about 26 years old. She thanked me and asked if "baby" was all right. The dear old soul's brain had dulled – she thought I was Father. They don't make people like that any more!'

Mr Vincent of Norwich is getting on for 80. He fondly remembers his no-nonsense grandmother who lived at Tivetshall in Suffolk. 'She was often called to lay a dead person out; she also helped out at childbirth. If a woman had milk fever she wouldn't hesitate to suck the milk off and spit it in the fire.' Desperate situations often called for desperate measures. Such action saved lives.

New mothers were well looked after, their every need catered for and their family looked after until they were considered strong enough to take over the running of their household again. Most home confinements lasted anything up to two weeks.

Mrs Durrant of Ipswich is in her eighties and remembers the arrangements. 'My son was born in 1935; my daughter in 1941. I had both at home. In those days we engaged a real homely local woman, very experienced (although not trained), always a natural mother and nearly always a widowed woman who was glad of the chance to go into somebody's home and earn by taking complete charge of the running of that home for approximately two weeks. She would do the washing and the cooking, allowing the new mother a week or ten days' complete rest after the birth. The district nurse or midwife took charge of the actual delivery and would enlist the doctor's advice or help if complications arose. Being a woman's natural function to bear children, this seldom happened. I was so happy being at home with the family, who were all, myself included, well cared for by the resident woman.

Young Mothers both

but —
the one tired and worn,
the other youthful and healthy.

Luck ? No, science made the difference.
Headaches, tiredness, loss of teeth and
hair, these symptoms, so often found
in young and expectant mothers, are
now known to be caused by a lack of
calcium in the blood.

More calcium than is obtained from
ordinary diet is an absolute necessity if
you do not want to suffer from those
complaints that so often rob a woman of
her bloom and freshness. With Kalzana,
the calcium food, you are safe. Kalzana
is easily taken up by the blood. It is a
food and not a drug.

*"Kalzana acts efficiently in protecting
the expectant and the nursing mother
against a dangerous loss of calcium,"*
writes the Medical Journal, "The
Practitioner."

Start taking Kalzana to-day, then you need not
fear the coming event. You will not only be a
happy but also a healthy young mother.

Kalzana

THE CALCIUM FOOD

At all Chemists at 2/9 & 4/11 per package.
Made by A. Wulfing & Co., Amsterdam, Holland.

Write for this Free Sample *Simply send us your address
with a 1½d. stamp (for postage)
and you will receive a sample*
tube of Kalzana with interesting booklet entirely free.
(Dept. W.H.J.), THERAPEUTIC PRODUCTS, LTD.,
NAPIER HOUSE, 24/27, HIGH HOLBORN, W.C.1.

Most of the mothers made life-long friends with these women.'

Nothing was left to chance. The pregnant mother was monitored closely by the midwife; a doctor's advice was sought if any problems arose or were expected. Morag Reed, who now lives in Colchester, only weighed six and a half stone before her pregnancy and the doctor was rather dubious about her pelvic measurements. 'In 1949 I had the chance of going into a small maternity home which was managed by three local doctors. I chose to have my baby at home – how right I was. The doctor called in at least three times from the third month of pregnancy and the midwife called in whenever she was passing.

'As time went on, the doctor was quite happy about a home delivery but ordered certain high standards of lighting in the bedroom and a similar standard of availability of hot water. He also wanted to be satisfied that the family would be on hand to help at the birth and for two weeks afterwards. Luckily we had a telephone or I think he would have ordered that too.

'Things went quicker than the midwife thought, and she called the doctor to administer gas and air, as only doctors were allowed to do then. The poor doctor arrived in his gardening clothes. My husband and my mother were kept out of the way by being asked to chain-pass hot water. I missed my husband's presence because in the early stages he had the marvellous knack of keeping the length of contractions controlled, merely by talking and keeping me calm. At one stage the doctor decided to call in a colleague as he was afraid his eyes were not good enough for an instrument delivery – this turned out to be unnecessary. He told me afterwards that having to call in another doctor had made up his mind that my son was his last baby. In his many years of military service in India during the first four decades of this century, he had helped deliver hundreds of babies.'

Mrs Reed had a quite different experience when she was forced to go into a maternity home two years later for the birth of her son. 'Their lack of amenities was dreadful. No doctor was at hand to help the girl in the next bed who became ill. A midwife had to cycle two miles in a storm to fetch help. Only a qualified midwife was available and the auxiliary staff were incredibly superstitious. "You must keep the baby bound up really tight," and "Don't cut the baby's nails, he will turn out a thief".'

Pregnancy was never treated as an illness, although most men would rather have faced a battle than have been forced into a delivery room. They did not always get their way at the end of nine months. One, now 80-year old, Suffolk lady scared the life out of her husband in the late 1930s. 'I was pottering about in the kitchen when my labour pains started. It was my first and I had been told that the pains could go on for hours. I was more intent on getting the house in order, preparing pots and pans for the hot water which would be needed. My husband was so nervous and got on my wick so I sent him out into the garden. About 20 minutes later things started to happen; I shouted to him for help. Luckily the neighbour had been out in his garden and when I shouted, he shouted for his wife. My neighbour's wife did a splendid job of delivering my baby, assisted by two very worried looking husbands.'

Having men in attendance was nothing new. Royalty always had a man in attendance who knew nothing about childbirth – a government minister had to be present to make sure everything was above board and that the new heir was the genuine one. The birth of Queen Victoria's eldest son in 1841 was attended by a Minister of State, Sir James Graham. Before withdrawing from the royal delivery room, where Her Majesty was discreetly concealed behind the curtains of a vast four-poster bed, Sir James congratulated the Queen on the birth of 'a very fine boy'. In a voice muffled by the heavy curtains, but true to her majestic personality, the Queen imperiously corrected, 'A very fine *prince*, Sir James!'

One hundred and seven years later, in 1948, the birth of Prince Charles could scarcely have been more different. It was, of course, an important occasion, of great public and political interest, yet true to the style which would mark the reign of Elizabeth II, it was essentially a family matter. King George VI abolished the ancient

tradition of having a government minister present at all royal births; his decision saved the Princess and Mr Chuter Ede, then Home Secretary, from what was undoubtedly an embarrassing situation.

I was born at home on January 31st 1942. Father was a cowman

near Norwich but he moved my mother to Stibbard near Fakenham a few weeks before my birth to be near some of his relatives,
as they lived on a houseboat at Trowse at the time and Hitler's
bombing raids were a concern. Father visited her every weekend
by bus from Norwich, but I was obviously so comfortable in my
mother's womb I decided to stay at least a month longer than the
expected birthdate. Mr Riches, a Stibbard farmer, heard of Dad's
plight and offered him a job. Dad took it. When my mother's
labour pains started, Dad had to cycle in snow in search of the
midwife. I've liked snow ever since! I was joined years later by two
more sisters. Jennifer was born at my paternal grandmother's house
in Stoke Holy Cross in 1944 and Shirley at the same house, in the
same front living room, six years later.

Women often went home to mother for the birth. Mrs Mollie
Goodyear of Sprowston near Norwich did just that. 'I had four
children, all born at home in 1954, 1956, 1959 and 1961. Two of
my children were born at my mother's house, a few minutes from
our prefab home. We had no telephone so my husband had to go
to the nearest telephone box. During one of my labours the doctor didn't come till the afternoon to give me a stitch because he
had been busy moving house.'

Doctors, it seems, quite enjoyed the home-birth experience.
Mrs Goodyear continues her story: 'One of my daughters was
born on August 1st at the start of the school holidays. Near my
time the doctor came in and said all was well, because I was still
waiting. He went downstairs and watched cricket with my husband. The midwife was getting near retirement and had said the
afternoon before, "I hope you won't call me in the night, as I've
had a few bad nights." I had to call her in at 3 am.'

Mollie is still amazed and quite concerned about the way today's
mothers are up and about in no time at all. 'We used to stay in bed
ten to twelve days and then felt so weak when we got up.'

Fiona Walker lives in the Suffolk countryside with her husband
Peter and two children. She is a modern-day mother and opted for
a home birth for her second child two years ago because her hos-

pital experience was far from satisfactory. She explains: 'My first labour was very long and I'm convinced, in part, that was because I was stressed by the fact that unless you produce a child within a certain amount of time of having the waters broken or a certain amount of time of saying your contractions actually started, they regard it as being a problem. They assume these days, that unless you have every test that's going, thing are going to be bad. Instead of assuming that everything is going to be fine unless otherwise proved.'

When Fiona discovered she was pregnant for the second time, she and Peter did not tell anyone. 'I have to emphasise that we knew all the potential risks but we don't see pregnancy in those terms. I don't see you need to look for risks. You need to be aware and read your body. Unfortunately, I had to tell the doctor because we were going overseas but I didn't have an ante-natal till I was 16 weeks pregnant. The doctor was reasonably understanding – he thought it a bit of a hoot. If you don't have a scan, many regard you as being completely potty or awkward. I decided not to have a scan with my second baby at all, I preferred not to. We specified at the time that if our child was born severely damaged or whatever happened, we would want it naturally fed. If it survived it did, and if it didn't, it didn't. I'd leave it to nature.'

Fiona and Peter had a wonderful experience of home birth six years ago. In fact, Fiona walked down the garden later that same day to hang out the washing. A little later she and Peter went shopping in the Safeway store at Beccles!

This modern-day story was inserted to give some indication of how short a time present-day mothers rest. Harold Reeder, in his nineties, used to live in the Lowestoft area. He makes the same comparison. 'My grandson, David, took his wife, Jane, into hospital in the early hours of the morning. He was present at the birth, helping where possible. At midday Jane's mother took their little daughter Nicole, aged three, to see her new baby brother. At four o'clock that afternoon, all the family were back home. So different to when I was a child. All babies were born at home. Mothers,

Mrs Barnard and one of her daughters, at the turn of the century, from the author's family album.

female friends and relatives would all rally round to help. Fathers and other menfolk were banished from the house. If the children were old enough they stayed to help, otherwise they went to a neighbour's house. Mother and baby would stay in bed for days, often it would be weeks before the new mother wheeled her new baby out in the pram.

'It was rather different in our household. There were four of us children, aged 19 down to me aged nine. In 1913 Mother had our new brother. A Mrs Mayhew, an established midwife, came to attend Mother and look after the rest of us in general. She came early, helped the doctor and stayed for *four* weeks. To us kids it seemed she stayed forever. She wore a white starched uniform and headdress. She crackled when she moved.

'She may have been very good in caring for Mother and baby Edward, but in the house she was severely lacking. She once put a pound of sausages into a saucepan of water, added two handfuls of flour and left it to boil over on the kitchen range. She plonked it on the kitchen table, spilling some – what a horrible mess. Weeping, she pleaded with us not to tell Dad. We helped her clean up but traces remained for ages. The final straw came when Dad returned from work one evening. Nurse Mayhew placed a large plate of fish before him. Dad made a motion with his hands – no knife or fork. Nurse crumpled up two sheets of newspaper and put one each side of Dad's plate. In horror, we watched as Dad picked up the paper, flung it on the floor, stamped on it and stormed out of the house.

'We didn't know what happened but Mother appeared soon after and Nurse Mayhew vanished forever. But always remembered.'

Fathers were nothing if not proud. Geoffrey Humphrey of Brantham, Suffolk was able to indulge his passion for hanging out the nappies yet again. 'The back bedroom of our railway cottage home overlooked a car park and the yard master's office. The doctor had insisted he be present at this delivery; judging by the midwife's attitude, she did not want him there. I needed to run a mile to the nearest telephone box but once the midwife had arrived I was given the minimum of time to contact the doctor. The timekeeper in the office kept a good look out for me and at a pre-arranged signal from our bedroom window contacted the doctor for me. I then rushed off as if to make a dash to the telephone box, instead I fled to the timekeeper's office for a cup of tea and a chat. In fairness to the midwife, she was great and delivered three lovely children for us. They were happy times. As chief-cook and bottle-washer I enjoyed washing and hanging out the nappies to declare another Humphrey had arrived.'

Times were hard for most during the early part of this century. The National Health Service did not come into being until 1948 so patients had to pay; separately for the midwife and nurse and again if the doctor was called. This 89-year old Suffolk lady wishes to remain anonymous: 'I was born in the East End of London. I married a countryman and lived in Suffolk where I had my first child in 1938 at the age of 30; my husband was 40. The district nurse delivered my baby whilst my husband cycled to the next village to get my aunt. The doctor had to be called as the afterbirth would not come away. I had to sign a form before he attended me as it was necessary to pay in those days.'

The experience of home birth was not all honey memories. Mrs Eva Holland who lives in Suffolk remembers being put off having babies as a teenager. 'My mother had a child in her forties at home. The doctor had to attend and she ended up with a prolapsed navel which meant she had to wear a special belt and pad.'

Gypsies were part of country life, too. They were often to be seen and like the rest of the population became pregnant, but it seems the niceties afforded others were not reserved for this race of people. One lady explains: 'Near our house was a lane where the gypsies sometimes stayed. One day the district nurse delivered a gypsy baby. I know she collected lots of newspapers before attending, presumably to use instead of wadding to keep the bed clean. Newspapers could be thrown away.'

Of course, the unexpected draws out the best in people. Earlier

The author and her son Martin, 1968.

this century life in the community was all about helping each other. Villagers relied heavily upon each other in times of need because communication was so poor. The amenities we take for granted today were not there; no telephones, no cars, no electricity supplies. Even underweight babies had to take their chances in a world which lacked luxury. Muriel Fall of Bures in Suffolk was fed liquor to keep her alive. 'My twin sister and I weighed less than 2lb each when we were born in February 1919. Although this was guesswork because the nurse did not have any scales to weigh us. We were premature and were not bathed for some weeks, only

gently washed over with olive oil. We were wrapped in a shawl near a hot water bottle next to our mother. We were kept alive with drops of brandy – the nurse went to the Manor House to get it; actually begging for it.'

Mothers were tough too. Mrs Rosemary Snowden of Cransford had four children, all born at home. 'With one of my babies I needed stitches. The nurse held my hand whilst the doctor did the stitching. I had no injection because the doctor said the injection would hurt as much as the stitches. He asked me to be brave and I was.'

Mrs Giles of Clacton-on-Sea writes: 'I had six children between 1940 and 1959. Three boys and three girls. My first daughter was born during an air raid. The midwife, summoned from a local telephone box, arrived on her bicycle through the air raid. I never attended a clinic till the fourth month of pregnancy. In my opinion, all this monitoring and scanning is dangerous to the unborn child. Most tend to forget that childbirth is a natural function provided one has led a healthy, sensible life.'

Mrs Giles, too, resorted to brandy. 'My eldest son was born prematurely in 1944, because of constant air raids. I had to feed him every two hours with glucose and brandy. Having a baby in the quiet of one's own home is far better all round; the baby only has the family germs to cope with. Nurses do not seem to wear masks any more either. The practice of inducing horrifies me. In my opinion there is no such thing as an overdue baby, provided it is still moving. They come when they are ready.'

Home births were real family affairs in more ways than one. Mrs Thatcher of Tunstall near Woodbridge recalls: 'I had all three children at home. The midwife walked five miles in fog and ice to deliver my son. My eldest was almost five when I had my second son. I didn't want to leave him by going into hospital. In fact, he walked into the bedroom with his hamster just as the baby was born. The midwife calmly told him she had three hamsters and she would see him and hamster downstairs in a couple of minutes. He shut the door and went downstairs to tell my husband, "The baby's out".'

Midwives were, on the whole, a cheerful bunch, very kind and caring. They came in all shapes and sizes, of course. Mrs Pippa Cornish of Buxhall near Stowmarket remembers hers. 'She was tiny in stature, drove a Mini car and was always accompanied by her wire-haired terrier dog. I sat on the edge of the bed praying she would arrive before the baby. She came and quickly whipped a plastic sheet over the mattress with the comment, "I've never lost a bed yet!".'

A retired Suffolk schoolteacher remembers a very special lady. Nobody in the Waveney Valley would forgive me for not mentioning her – Nurse Mattocks. A big lady with a heart and a voice to match, she sallied forth with brute confidence. He laughs at the memory: 'She was a real character with a no-fuss approach. When she arrived to deliver one of our children she asked for lots of brown paper. I was curious. "I want to put it around the walls, I'm a messy blighter at work!" After the baby was safely delivered she came to me in the kitchen with a newspaper parcel under her arm. "Now git rid of this." It was the afterbirth and I was at a loss to know what to do with it.'

Another patient recalls: 'One day she came and examined me because I was in labour. She told me I was not ready. "Shove over," she said, "I've had a busy day and can do with some kip." She slept for an hour beside me. It was a great comfort to know that she was there.'

Many will remember the old wives' tale about the afterbirth. When it burned, it popped – according to how many times it popped that was the number of extra children that particular mother could expect. It came true on many occasions!

Well, the women have had their say, what about the doctor? Dr P. Rawlence of Pulham Market near Diss is a man with amusing memories: 'Betty was a big bonny 19-year-old. One Sunday morning I was called out to the village. Betty was having tummy pains and when I arrived, her mother, a small bird-like woman, was hovering around anxiously. It didn't take me long to determine the cause of Betty's trouble. Turning to mother I said, "Mrs

M…, in about 20 minutes' time you are going to be a grandmother!" I shall never forget the look on her face. Dumbfounded!
Thunderstruck! Gobsmacked! All rolled into one. She stood there
for what seemed an age but was probably just a few seconds. Then,
as though to the manner born, she had pulled out a drawer, lined
it with clean warm towels, heated the water in the copper and
there we were, all set to receive the lovely baby girl within the pre-
dicted 20 minutes. Betty married soon after and the unexpected
arrival is now a mother of three.

'In the same village a year or two later, Beryl came from London
with her husband and two children. Sadly, her husband, who had
heart trouble, died not long after. Beryl, still a very attractive
young woman, courted and married a good local man, always
reckoned to be a confirmed bachelor. Beryl became pregnant and
all went well till her time was due. Another urgent call came from
the village, for both doctor and midwife. Beryl had started and I
beat the midwife to the scene. However, in spite of my rapid
response, it was what we in the trade called a BBA, ie born before
arrival of doctor or midwife. A fine boy lay protesting loudly at
this precipitate arrival into the world, still attached to the umbilical
cord. Beryl gazed up at me from the bed and I shall never forget
the look on her face. "I'm sorry, doctor," her appealing eyes brim-
ming with tears. "I'm sorry doctor, I just stood up and out 'e
come".'

So many lovely recollections, but I've saved the best till last.
Each generation has its special memories and children are no
exception. Ena Dye of Fakenham shares some treasured thoughts
with us: 'Being the eldest child in the family by some four years, I
can remember my three sisters and brother being born at home
between the years 1934 and 1949. Laying awake at night (most
were born at night, or so it seems), hearing that first cry and then,
"Come and see your new sister." Sitting on the bed close to Mum
and being allowed to hold this new life; "Be gentle now, give her a
kiss." The smell of disinfectant, nurse in her crisp white apron
rustling while she beamed from a great height. Mum and Dad

Maria Clears, from the author's family album.

looking so proud. Such a glow of love, warmth and of feeling safe; it lives with me still. Nurse Shipabottom of Lowestoft – in the end our midwife and family friend.'

> Monday's child is fair of face,
> Tuesday's child is full of grace.
> Wednesday's child is full of woe,
> Thursday's child has far to go.
> Friday's child is loving and giving,
> Saturday's child works hard for a living.
> But the child that is born on the Sabbath Day,
> Is bonny, and blithe, and good, and gay.

Right and Wrong

—— ❦ ——

'The local bobby had the parents' permission to tick you off with a clout around the ear and, worse, he might threaten to tell your mother or father. His ticking off was bad enough, but Mother's! Oh dear, it didn't bear thinking about.'

'Children should be seen and not heard' – how many children complained about that old adage a few years ago? Very few, they just wouldn't dare because Father or Mother's word was law. Disobey at your peril!

Many might question the wisdom of such strict rules but it must be remembered families were large and control difficult enough. There were often some tough little rats amongst the members, who, left to their own devices, would have played havoc on the nerves of the whole family. Discipline was therefore harsh for a reason. It was necessary to maintain order of course, but discipline also went hand-in-hand with good manners. The one complemented the other. Parents were keen to give their children the best and social acceptance was more important than a state of mind.

Children were made to feel responsible for their actions and fully aware of the consequences. Mr Cook of Woodbridge recalls one incident when he was a roguish youngster: 'I had pinched Father's bicycle for a little trip rather than walk. He was at work and I thought he'd be none the wiser. I managed a puncture on the way home but put the bike back exactly where I'd found it. "You may be clever but not clever enough for me. And don't forget I'm bigger than you!" he snapped at the tea table. Suffice to say, he did not look radiant. Without further ado he whipped my plate away, gave me a clout and sent me off to bed without any tea.'

Now that may seem harsh punishment for a rather light crime but it showed there was little leeway for misbehaviour of any sort. Fathers, particularly, were more firm than friendly. Maurice Winter of Gorleston remembers: 'My mother was born on 30th July 1898. Her name was May Alice Edwards. Her father, George Henry Edwards, was lucky enough and clever enough to get a job with Norwich Union Life Office in which he progressed very well. A hard worker, always ready to help juniors, he would come down like ton of bricks on anyone who was slacking on the job. He had a great facility with figures (I believe he was taught his multiplication tables up to 20 x 20) and became treasurer of the Congregational church at Chapelfield, Norwich. He was extremely straight-laced, teetotal and a non-swearer. If he made a minor mistake he could sometimes be heard to say "Dash" but if he were really exasperated he would exclaim "Tar that pig".

'May Alice became a very athletic, lissom little girl. Mostly she enjoyed good health but when she was about five or six she had some minor childish malady, for which the doctor prescribed some extremely nasty medicine. Those were the days when all medicine was nasty and the nastier it was, apparently the better it was. One day George Henry sent May Alice to the scullery to take her medicine. Instead of taking the medicine, May Alice poured out the dose and put it down the sink. George Henry asked, "Now May, have you taken your medicine?" She replied, "Yes, Dada." Unknown to May Alice, George Henry had been watching her through a crack in the door, and he flew into a tremendous rage. He thrashed her and thrashed her until she howled. It was very painful. May Alice really did think this was over the top; however, she never told a lie again; furthermore it left her with a lifelong hatred and contempt for liars.'

Of course, there were varying degrees of strictness. Sometimes the father left the punishing to mother and that was no joke. Some mothers could make even the biggest and strongest of lads quiver in fright.

*Loving discipline did not curb high spirits too much − the author (right)
with her sister Jennifer performing handstands for Mum, 1951.*

My own grandmother would never be crossed. She raised almost enough children for a football team. My father is 79 years old and the eldest of nine, all still surviving with the exception of one daughter.

He remembers how she sorted the six boys out once. 'I can't remember what we had done at the time because we were a robust bunch, but she tied us all to chairs. We did not dare speak, let alone try and set ourselves free.' She loved all her children but was remorseless in punishment if they disobeyed.

All this discipline generally came with a lot of love and care, One gentleman, Mr Dawson from Fakenham, speaks well of Mother's influence too. 'Mother was the dictator in our family. We were always taught to understand the consequences of our actions. By the time we grew up we were well equipped to deal with life's ups and downs and what's more had a sense of real worth; even if our employment was as mundane as emptying the weekly cesspit!'

Ron Deacon of Northwold in Norfolk remembers his child-hood well: 'Although I got many a chiding from my mum, I still had a very happy childhood in a very loving Christian home.' I wrote to him after noticing a letter he had sent to the editor of our local daily, the *Eastern Daily Press*, following an article about the former air base at Watton which was employing security guards 24 hours a day to patrol the site in an attempt to stop children going in there. 'I am a bit puzzled. Why cannot the parents just tell their children to keep away from the area. If I, as a child, had dared to disobey my mum, the hurt I would have got from her would have exceeded anything that the hazards of the old air base could do.'

And if youngsters thought that being away from the home spelt freedom, they were very much mistaken. The local bobby was always riding about his beat on a cycle and if he caught you doing something you shouldn't it was as bad as being branded from the pulpit. He would have had the parents' permission to tick you off with a clout around the ear, and, worse, he might threaten to tell your mother or father. His ticking off was bad enough, but Mother's! Oh dear, it didn't bear thinking about.

Gaining a sense of freedom in the workplace didn't help matters. When my father left school at the age of 14 in 1932 he was living with his maternal grandmother who needed a strong boy around the place, since she was a widow. It was necessary for Dad to hand over his wage packet each week to his grandmother. He earned ten shillings a week and his grandmother gave him one shilling back as spending money. They lived in Stoke Holy Cross near Norwich. One night some of his mates were cycling to the cinema in Norwich. They asked my father to join them and told him they were thinking of taking some girls. He would need half a crown. He borrowed the money from his none-too-happy grandmother. He cycled to Norwich all right but was so afraid of spending the money, that he refused to go in the cinema and cycled home with the money still intact. He laughs at the memory, 'I knew damn well if I had spent that money I would have got a slap of the skull.'

Marriage did not let some of these tough boys off the hook either. They only had to cause a marital commotion and Mother would come to the assistance of her daughter-in-law. Mother was not always the sweet-tempered lady in the clean pinny!

Education and Schooldays

'Git yar hid outa that thar book, boy, and do somethin' useful for a change!'

'**Y**ou know, I am not happy with your school report,' little
Johnnie's father stated.

'Nor was my teacher. I don't know why she sent it home,' little
Johnnie exclaimed.

This sort of joke was quite common a few decades ago. Education was obligatory, of course, but as long as the pupils could read and write at the end of their educational years, it was considered sufficient to carry any child through life. In fact, it was considered much more useful if the child was accomplished in gardening, because knowledge in this area alone would result in their having something on the table at meal times.

Harold I. Reeder of Leicester is in his nineties. He lived and was educated in Pakefield near Lowestoft as a child. He left school at the age of 14 and went into an engineering factory where he worked a 55-hour week. He is an intelligent man with an astute brain but recalls: 'There were a lot of very ignorant people about in my young days, especially in the countryside. Many school-age children who lived in the country had to help out on farms and so missed a lot of schooling.'

'Education was almost a dirty word in some families,' recalls Mrs Porter of Lowestoft. It was all very well to enjoy reading but it didn't get the work done, did it? 'Git yar hid outa that thar book, boy, and do somethin' useful for a change.' This sort of admonishment was very real.

Children outside Stibbard school in 1900.

Whilst the word 'dunce' was nothing to be proud of, an intellectual man from a poor background was an embarrassment to all. Scholarly children who wore spectacles lived through some very bad patches. The clowns of the classroom would make life a misery for such children by jeering 'Four Eyes!' Those with more than an average knowledge were ridiculed as 'Big Head'.

One lady who went to school in the 1930s remembers how she failed to produce good work. 'I couldn't see the blackboard properly and so found the lessons very difficult. It was a great worry for me but I didn't dare admit this weakness. I dreaded the idea of spectacles.'

Many spoke about the effects of being left-handed. Trying to write with the left hand was a punishable offence in many cases. 'Many is the time I got a slap around the ear because I was writing with my left hand,' stated one elderly gentleman. 'It was only when I went up a class to a teacher who possessed some understanding that I was allowed to use the hand I felt more happy with.'

Mr Donald Neave of Attleborough has been researching village life in Long Melford during the years 1920 to 1930. He writes: 'Earlier this century education was controlled by expenditure; largely determined by the will of local councils, which in rural areas were controlled by persons whose main objective was to control expenditure. Many of these die-hards were people who did not believe in education for the masses; at the most they conceded that a sufficiency of basic learning was all that was required to enable future workers to do their job more effectively. Attendance at elementary schools was compulsory. In the main, grammar-type schools were fee-paying schools and up until the 1930s a few free places were awarded as a result of examination. A considerable number of fee-paying pupils would not have passed the examination but the parents were only really interested in obtaining a grammar school label for their children. There is no doubt that many very able children were not allowed to sit the free place examination, possibly because of short-sightedness on behalf of their parents who could not afford the school uniform or simply because a wage-earner would be lost for some years. Up until 1918 some pupils qualified to leave as early as 14 in order to earn – so you see the provision of opportunity for self-advancement or self-fulfilment just did not come into the decision. It was quite outside the consideration of most people.'

Some parents did get pleasure from the opportunities which presented themselves to their children. Mr Roy Larkins of Lowestoft remembers when he qualified for a local grammar school place earlier this century. 'My mother immediately went to the mother of a much older boy already at the grammar school and came back with a very secondhand school blazer, school cap and tie; and she spent all that night stitching up the elbows of the blazer.'

In the early 1930s all pupils wishing to go to grammar (or county secondary modern) school had to sit an examination at the age of eleven. The parents of those passing would have to be means-tested to determine the fees to be paid. Before the Second World War only a very small number of leavers went on to further education, university or technical college. Many local education authorities did not give grants for advanced courses, so many children with potential just did not get the chance for further education.

Those who were fortunate enough to get to grammar school had to make great sacrifices with their time. Marjorie Ling (nee Stimpson) lives at Carleton Rode near Norwich. Born in Diss on 7th November 1919, her family moved to Harleston when she was six years old. 'I won the scholarship examination to take up secondary education. I travelled to Beccles on the 8 am train, returning at 6.45 pm. I had to walk the mile and a half from Beccles station to get to the Sir John Leman School. School lessons finished at 3.30 pm but as there was no train back 'til 6 pm, I had to stay at school until 5.30 pm. I would do my homework under the eagle eye of the master or mistress on duty, then walk to the station to catch the train home, arriving at Harleston station at 6.45 pm.'

Grammar schools were expected to offer a little more than a good education. Strength of character was also a feature built into grammar education.

Mr R. F. Lawrence lives at Wroxham near Norwich. He is 88 years old and hopes to write a sequel to the book he had published on his 80th birthday. His book *The Dumpling's Tale* carries a passage on his grammar school days: 'Life at the grammar school was a very different proposition from the village school. During the winter time we had to keep our overcoats on as the school fires were not lit until just before classes commenced. The school had a cadet corps which all boys in reasonable health were expected to join. The ex-army character in charge, fresh from his spell in the 1914–1918 war, made sure that our standard of drilling, and knowledge of weaponry, was first class.

'Certainly that standard prevailed throughout the school, as the masters and one mistress knew their job, and made sure that we attained a standard of excellence which would not let the school down when it came to exam time. There was a system of penalty points for misbehaviour or shoddy workmanship. Anything over two points in a week meant a visit to the headmaster who, in a kindly manner, would lecture us on our deficiencies and, if in his opinion we deserved it, we would get six or more strokes of the cane, which made sitting down uncomfortable at times. The school maintained a good reputation on the sports field. I passed the normal end-of-school leaving examination at the age of 15, with a number of credits and an additional scholarship to boot. I had to forego the scholarship, which would have eventually taken me on to public school, because my father was very ill at the time and it was necessary for me to leave and find a job. We had a small farm; my older brother had already left grammar school early to look after the farm and, of course, I was expected to do my bit.'

Until the early 1950s village children attended the same school, from beginning to end of their education. Usually it had two large school rooms, 'the little room' and 'the big room'. The head teacher presided over 'the big room', sometimes assisted by pupil teachers – children who had stayed on at the school with a view to eventually becoming a teacher. They would help in the school and study for their preliminary certificate, which was approximately the equivalent of the present GCSE. Upon passing this and having reached the age of 18, they would be recognised by the, then, Board of Education as uncertified teachers. Others coming from grammar schools would spend a year as a student teacher under the head's supervision. At the end of the year they would be recognised as uncertified teachers. Uncertified teachers then went on to a teachers' training college to become certified teachers.

I can personally vouch for the effectiveness of village schools. I started at Stoke Holy Cross village school in 1947, at the age of five. We had a 'little room' and a 'big room'. Miss O'Mara was the headmistress; she had taught my father years earlier. I had some uncles in the big room; I was a shy thing and they took the mickey out of me – I must say in a quite charming way. Belonging to my family, it was necessary to harden up quickly because a lot of well-mannered tormenting went on. Each room was heated, in winter, by a large open fireplace, surrounded by a heavy black iron guard.

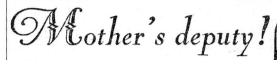

The teacher, naturally, sat at her desk at one side of the fireplace. In fact, dear Miss O'Mara would often gently lift the back of her skirt when we were at work, in order to warm her backside. I always thought this a great privilege and copied this luxury at home. To be recommended!

The whole school integrated itself into one big and, I say, happy family. But do not think for one moment discipline was lax. Quite the opposite. The two teachers were adamant when it came to maintaining order. In fact, in the big room, Miss O'Mara was never without a ruler in her hand. Big boys, and I mean rumbustious big country lads, knew much better than to ruffle her feathers! She was mean with a ruler and it came down hard when pupils were least expecting it. As one ex-pupil stated: 'She could tame lions with her ruler!'

Needless to say, I respected both teachers and never did get the ruler or cane. Old goody two-shoes has changed colour since then!

They were happy days and I put love of nature down to the weekly nature walks we had, along the banks of the river Tas. We would happily stand around teacher out in the open as ordered, for another nature explanation. We brought back leaves and the fruits of the trees, and once inside the classroom we would pin these samples onto thick paper and write a little passage on our venture. I absolutely adored these lessons. In fact, most children in the class could name trees by just looking.

Our teachers were unmarried, as was usual in those days, and so tended to treat the class as their own children, or so I always felt. Great effort and endeavour went into preparation for lessons. These teachers went even further at Christmas time because each pupil received a wrapped Christmas present.

Phil Colman remembers his schooldays: 'I remember when a teacher lost control of our class in 1926 and we kids went on strike. It had to happen because we took no notice of him. When he threatened us with the cane, we kicked him in the shins. When he left the room once we put every pencil down holes in the wooden floor so that when he came back in there was not a pencil to be had in the class.

'He retired and another male teacher came. On his first day we all assembled in class. He stood up and bellowed, "Who is the head boy?" One of the burliest stood up. The new teacher said, "I want you to go outside and cut one of the biggest lengths of cane from that bush. This is my first day here and I have to go to a funeral. You will be in charge of the cane. If any of the class misbehaves you have my authority to cane them." The boy proudly did as he was ordered. The headmaster then called the infants teacher in. "I want you to take down the names of any pupil who misbehaves or acts in an unorderly manner."

'Before he left he said, "Now you can do what you want today. You can read, write, go outside in the playground. Anything you fancy as long as you behave." He then stared at two very ugly-tempered boys in the class who had in the past been responsible for much of the trouble. He beckoned them over. "Just to make sure

A typical classroom of the early 1900s, at Old Catton, near Norwich.

you behave I'm going to punish you now." Without further ado, he banged their heads together. He left them bawling their eyes out. When he came back from the funeral he went to the infants teacher. She had not had cause to write down a single name. The class had not been a mite of trouble.'

Mr Colman goes on: 'We had a good all-round education but when I left I could not spell. I always got top marks for composition and sums, but I never could spell. The headmaster told my mother, "He'll do alright in life, no harm will come to him. He's the craftiest little humbug I've ever known!"'

Many children found earning a penny or two much more interesting and worthwhile than sitting in a classroom all day. David Vincent is 48 years old and lives in Raveningham, Norfolk. He works on a local farm and has worked in agriculture since leaving school. As a child he lived with his family at Holly Farm, Thurlton. He attended Thurlton village school. 'Mrs Ridley was the headmistress. During the sugar beet season I helped father load the once-a-month lorry load. We loaded the beet by shovel. I skipped school this day, preferring instead a lorry ride to Cantley sugar beet factory. I liked earning; from the age of eleven I helped every school holidays in the harvest on Lord Somerleyton's estate near Lowestoft.'

A lot of this sort of truancy went on. But it must be said that children only missed school because they chanced upon an opportunity to earn money.

Working before and after school was quite normal in some families. Mr Cook of Hethersett is 85 years old, a semi-retired farmer, who attended Bungay Grammar School. 'I had to walk one and a half miles to and from school each day, in all weathers. When I was eleven I was hand-milking twelve cows before I went to school and twelve cows when I got back home. It was expected of me; if I was going to follow in Father's footsteps as a farmer I needed the experience. Mind, I loved every minute of it.'

Frank Howes was a milkman in the Lowestoft area in the 1920s. As a young boy, he never missed an opportunity to earn money. By

the age of twelve, Frank was working on a farm during his out-of-school hours. He went right through the farm calendar undertaking exhausting work, often with the cart horses. During the harvest-time school holidays he would be working in the fields all day. At the age of 13, Frank was introduced to a dairyman who asked him to deliver milk after school; Frank cycled around the area with a gallon can of milk on his handlebars, delivering to customers. On Saturdays and Sundays young Frank helped the dairyman with his morning milk round. Needless to say, when Frank left school at 14 he was taken on full time.

Of course, education did suffer, because some minds were more practical than studious. Take young Peter who attended a Norfolk village school in the 1940s. He was forever taking time out to work. At nine years old he was an accomplished handyman and could do practically anything with his hands, except hold a pencil properly!

The teacher decided to give this diligent little chap extra tuition because he was badly behind with his spelling. On a large square of cardboard she drew a lovely cat and underneath wrote 'CAT' in big letters. Time and again she held this card under Peter's nose, in an effort to impress the word in his memory. This went on for two or three days. Finally the test – teacher covered up the picture and showed Peter the word 'CAT'.

'Now what does this word say, Peter?' she asked pleasantly.

Without further ado and full of confidence, little Peter replied, 'Pussy!'

This is a perfectly true story and it shows the gap between the importance of work and school for some, at that time. As one intelligent man recalls, 'I felt that every minute I was at school I was wasting time. There were a hundred things calling out for my attention, all of which would earn me cash.'

During the Second World War, in 1944, Parliament passed the Education Act – one of the great landmarks in education. Grants for further education in university and technical college now had to be made to qualifying students, so a young person from the poorest home could fulfil his or her ambition. The biggest change brought about was the granting of equal status to all schools. Secondary (grammar) and elementary were no longer treated as separate sections of the education system. Gradually new, modern and more spacious buildings came into being. All unqualified teachers with 20 years' or more experience, were instantly pronounced qualified teachers.

By now, parents were becoming more interested in their children's education. They urged and pushed to get them through the eleven-plus examination. They realised a grammar school education would secure them more desirable jobs.

Rural society, however, lagged somewhat behind, as my own experience shows. I passed the eleven-plus examination but was sent to Loddon secondary modern school, which was closer to home, rather than a grammar. I was expected to be like most of the other girls. Meet a nice hard-working farm-hand, sooner rather than later, marry him and live happy ever after, presumably in the kitchen!

Which was fine by me; I loved school but had never had any pressure put on me to attain anything other than personal happiness. I loved coming home from school, changing my clothes and going out to play with my sisters, friends and pets. During all my years of education there was never a sheet of homework in sight. In short, I had a wonderfully active childhood free of any mental pressure. My head was clear – my body lithe and active. I could climb a tree as well, if not better, than the next child. We were all as free as birds.

I had no trouble securing my first job when I left school at the age of 15 in 1957, either. For some reason, if anybody asked me what I wanted to do when I left school, I always gave the same answer, 'A waitress!'

However, a few weeks before I was due to leave, the headmaster announced in assembly that Loddon Engineering were looking for two young ladies to work in their office. I decided to apply and so went to see the school secretary. An interview was arranged, I was

accepted at interview and started my training on Saturday mornings at Loddon Engineering prior to leaving school, in order to
train as a telephonist/receptionist-cum-postgirl. I instantly fell in
love with my plug-in switchboard.

After leaving school, I enrolled at my ex-school for evening
classes in typing and shorthand. It was all done through choice and
a thoroughly exciting time I had at work. I was not the exception
by any means. Many others sacrificed a grammar school education
for the very same reasons but still went on to fulfil themselves in
the work-place. Ah! but enthusiasm and dedication took one a
long way in those far off days.

What about discipline? Was there any secret? It seems the ruler
prevented most upsets; if that failed then there was always the cane.
'You have been warned several times!' Lines were the worst. Big
boys shivered horribly when they had to stay in at playtimes and
after school, to complete their lines. And these did not come in
tens, but hundreds. Neither ill health or bad weather got you out
of these.

Some parents did react if their little Sunny Jim was threatened.
My father recalls his schooldays in 1931. Apparently, one set of
parents were quite put out when their son got the cane as punishment. The pupil felt obliged to mention this next day. 'Chissie',
the headmaster, had the perfect answer. 'If they won't allow you to
take the punishment, perhaps next time they'd like to come along
and take the punishment for you.'

Mrs Gilbert of Felixstowe remembers her school days in the
1940s: 'The cane only served to enforce laid down rules. Teachers
were, after all, only trying to do their jobs well, which was to give
an education which would serve the pupils well in their future
lives. Of course, children cannot always see this but at our school
we were made to understand that any discipline was for our bene-
fit. In fact, trouble was nipped in the bud before it had a chance to
fester into something worse.'

A sense of duty was sown into the minds of children from a very
early age. Life, for ordinary families, was not easy and so children

The old village school at Raveningham, Norfolk, on the Raveningham estate. It was closed some years ago, but note the school house next door where the headmistress lived.

were expected to shoulder some of the responsibility. Most children who belonged to big families had daily chores to undertake; every member was expected to pull their weight. The following are a few jobs that some undertook:

'I was the eldest of ten and had to dress and breakfast the two youngest before I left for school each morning.'

'My mother was not well and when I was eight it was my job to fill three large pails with water out of the pump, before I left each morning.'

'When I returned from school I had to help with the main cooked meal of the day. This started when I was seven years old and continued until I left at the age of 14.'

My own father lived with his grandmother when she was widowed. She needed a strong boy about the place to help, and to fetch and return the washing which she took in to eke out the budget.

Some youngsters were raised most severely. A Norfolk lady, in her mid-fifties, looks back to her young days with a lot of bitterness. 'Mother was pregnant with me when Father went off to war. I was almost school-age when he returned; we all found it difficult to adjust. Up until his return I had Mother all to myself; suddenly this disciplinarian ruled our lives. Mother was frightened of him and I seemed to take the blame for everything. When I was six years old I had to help him feed his pigs after school. The pigs were fed on potatoes – it was my job to take off the shoots and put the potatoes into a big hopper. When it was full I had to hand pump it full of water; it was necessary for me to stand on a stool to see over the top and gauge how full the hopper was. Dad then boiled them all up. I was frightened to death of the pigs which made a lot of noise. If I complained all I got was, "If you don't shut up, I'll throw you into the pigs." When I reached the age of ten he decided I was old enough to help him saw wood. We had a double-handed saw which we pulled backwards and forwards across the logs. I had to put the logs in an old pram and push them home where I stockpiled them for winter. By the time I reached my teens I was helping him with the straw-stack.'

This lady worked her way through her childhood and to this day is an exceptionally determined and hard-working person.

As if working at such a tender age was not bad enough, pupils had to walk to school, often miles, in all weathers. The small niceties of life we take for granted now, like cars and school buses, just did not exist. There was no room for sensitivity here; the only bit of comfort was a companion in the shape of a brother or sister. Rugged up tightly against the harsh reality of winter, children were wide awake when they got to school and ready to sit still in the warmth of the classroom for their lessons. Ah! the blessing of good thick hand-knitted gloves, hats and scarves, not to mention jumpers and cardigans!

Summer time was no hardship as Mrs Blowers of Ipswich recalls:

'There were ten of us in the 1950s who walked one and three quarter miles to school each day. We were able to amuse ourselves along the journey by watching out for wild animals. We were sometimes early enough to even take a rest along the way; one of our party was always singing. It was something we had to do and we made the best of it.' Of course, traffic was apparent by its absence, The car was still in its infancy as far as owning one went. 'We had the whole road to ourselves most of the time. An occasional car would pass which was an amusement in itself. Some of us carried little notebooks and logged the registration numbers down. It was a fascinating hobby. It would take a week or more to fill even a small page of car registration numbers, depending how often one wished to sacrifice playing time by sitting on the roadside in wait.'

Mr Barber of Saxmundham talks about his schooldays in the early 1940s: 'There was little fuss or preparation about getting to school. Looking back, we were tough little blighters. We always got up in good time to eat breakfast and help Mother in any way we could before we left. The weather was no excuse for staying away either. Winters always seemed long and hard; if we had pandered to conditions we would never have gone. Mind, I had the odd day or two off when it snowed, mainly to help clear the pathways of our house and for neighbours who had no man about the place. I remember one particularly heavy snowfall when we were walking to school. One kid fell in a deep drift right up to his chest. We hauled him out and by the time we got to school he was virtually frozen stiff. The headmistress made him take off his outer garments, socks and boots. She hung the wet clothing around the big fire and it was ready for him when it was time to return home.'

Before the introduction of school meals in the mid 1940s, there was nothing more than cold water to drink during the day, so the pupils often took their own favourite beverages. Some took Bovril, others tea or cocoa with the required amount of sugar. The headmistress provided hot water and tin mugs at lunch time. Some children could not wait. My own father took a quantity of cocoa and sugar daily to school. 'It never ever got as far as school because

Old outside school toilets at Norton Subcourse. The contents were emptied onto the school gardens once a week.

I tucked into it, neat, before we got there. I loved the taste of cocoa and sugar.'

Lessons could sometimes be a good excuse to take life easy. I so enjoyed the special BBC lessons for school, when articulate broadcasters' voices would lull the class into a lovely sense of well-being. I can't remember what form these lessons took, but sufficient to say, the whole classroom relaxed in the silence of the headmistress, who sat at her desk just as peacefully as we did at ours. So precious were those 'on air' lessons that if any pupil dared make a noise and arouse the headmistress, the rest of the class punished that disruptive pupil with horrible stares.

However, 'Miss' had her uses at times. One late afternoon lesson a week she treated us to a story. The lulling effect on our brains when 'Miss' read to us was great. She didn't seem to mind what position individuals adopted as long as they kept quiet and listened, which was no hardship. Many simply folded their arms on the desk top and lay down their heads. It was all some of us could do to stay awake. When the story came to an end many would try and cajole her into an extra passage or two, 'Oh, please Miss, one more page, please.'

On the question of excessive tiredness, 'the little room' at Stoke Holy Cross was blessed with a mattress in one corner of the room, where very young children could take a nap if they so wished. Education was not blind to the energy expended in getting to school.

Routine played an important part in our school week. One afternoon saw the boys out in the school garden, growing vegetables. The last hour on a Friday afternoon was devoted to cleaning out our desks and arranging everything neatly for Monday morning. This time was not appreciated by the boys but until it had been carried out they were not allowed to leave. We girls used this time self-righteously, our efforts signified our aptitude for cleanliness. We were also handed polish for the desk tops; an industrious lot we were on a Friday afternoon. Once the inkwells were filled and clean blotting paper laid out, it was time for home and the week-end. Flashing smiles galore!

Looking back, schooldays were a lot of fun.

Marriage – A Woman's Career

⟨⟩

'Your new life will include housekeeping, perhaps a job, entertaining, social life and – last but not least – lovely quiet evenings at home with your husband' – Woman magazine 1954.

Somebody once said, 'Marriage has many pains, but celibacy has no pleasures!'

The following offering is a true tale. Tom and Daphne, in the mid-1920s, had been courting for nigh on 20 years. Tom was a farm labourer and Daphne was a kitchenmaid. They lived in the same Norfolk village. 'I think we ought to get married,' Daphne ventured after another goodnight kiss on her parents' front doorstep. Tom rubbed his stubbled chin, then remarked in a serious mood, 'A good idea…but who would have us?'

Marriage was a serious business, so much so that all mothers primed their daughters from birth. They taught them to knit, sew and cook as soon as they could co-ordinate their little fingers. These assets were invaluable to a woman because men were the breadwinners and women the home-makers. The duty and burden of keeping the family warm and well-fed fell on the housewife. My own father is the eldest of nine children and recalls that 'Mother used to cook *all* the meals on an open fire in the living room.'

So important was it to be married that the higher social classes sent their daughters off to finishing school, where they were taught how to smile, how to small-talk, how to entertain and how to look lovely – all day long.

You see, marriage was a career. A season ticket to freedom and choice no other career could offer. True career opportunities were limited for women. Most shop assistant positions were filled by men. Nurses and school-teachers had to be single, because, it was thought, it was impossible to be both married and to work satisfactorily. The following are some of the rules which applied to women teachers in 1915:

(a) You will not marry during the term of your contract.
(b) You are not to keep company with men.
(c) You may not loiter in ice-cream parlours.
(d) You may not smoke cigarettes.
(e) You may not dress in bright colours and you may not dye your hair.
(f) You must wear at least two petticoats and your dresses must be no shorter than two inches above the ankle.
(g) You must sweep the schoolroom floor at least once daily, clean the blackboard at least once and start the fire at 7 am.

Most of the available jobs for women were in the domestic field. Mrs Barker of Felixstowe is 83 years old and when she was twelve was sent off to a big house as a scullery maid. 'I was so homesick and hated my job. I only came home one Sunday a month. The work was pure drudgery. I was up at 5 o'clock in the morning, lighting fires all over the house in winter; I seemed to spend all my days washing, scrubbing and cleaning. There were four great big doors in that house and I had to scrub the huge steps every day, summer and winter alike.' Mrs Barker did not finish her tasks till 7 o'clock at night. 'I was too tired to do anything other than perhaps write a letter home, wash and get into bed.'

Marriage, in short, offered freedom from the hard world outside. It also offered respectability and a position in life, even if you were very poor. Being 'left on the shelf' was the one great terror. The humiliation of not being engaged by the time one was in the mid twenties was almost too much to bear for some. Unless one had the protection of a good, reasonably well-off family behind them whereby the single lady could be employed at home, the alternatives to marriage were quite unattractive.

After the First World War there were not enough young men to go round, so many having lost their lives fighting for their country. It goes without saying that 'spinsters' were thick on the ground. Their situation was not by choice. I spoke to many such ladies and the majority told me, through still misted eyes, that their 'young men' had been killed in the war. Many of these gentle ladies had never really got over the bad stroke of luck which had denied them the pleasures of lasting romance and children of their own.

Most young women planned their wedding day before they had even had a boyfriend. Collecting for the 'bottom drawer' was started as soon as the first wage packet was earned.

It was not easy to meet the man of your dreams, either. Unless he happened to live next door – and many unions were formed as a result – it was necessary to rely on introductions. Family and friends played a big part here. If a certain young lady expressed an interest in a certain young man, every effort was made to introduce the couple. Of course, some were introduced by accident and 'hit it off' immediately, although the relationship did not always live up to the 'for better or worse' vows.

A lady from Suffolk who wishes to remain anonymous explained to me: 'I married during the Second World War. My husband was on leave from the army and a friend introduced us. We married rather quickly as he was being sent away. He left me pregnant and lonely. He was away for a few years and when he returned we both realised we had made a dreadful mistake. We abstained from marital relations because I didn't love him. He had many love affairs during our married life. It didn't really bother me because I became active in local circles. Our daughter was a real treasure. I can't really say I missed a man's love all that much

The author's father and mother, Samuel and Violet Borrett, on their wedding day in May 1939.

because I had so many interests. He looked after us as a family financially and the marriage plodded on until he died some years ago. To this day nobody knows what a disaster romance-wise, the marriage was.'

On the whole, marriages were happy because the alternatives were so dire to even contemplate. Employment in the first part of this century was hardly an outlet for creative energy. Marriage, on the other hand, lent great scope for the artistically minded woman. There were clothes to be designed and made, either by sewing or knitting, cushions and tablecloths to be embroidered, curtains to be made, interior decoration to be planned.

Of course, shotgun weddings were a sudden headache to many parents, often because nobody came to terms with matters of a sexual nature until it was too late. The facts of life were never explained. Most young couples made do with 'heavy petting', canoodling which stopped short of actual intercourse. Sex before marriage was taboo. One gentleman confirms, 'The only way to get a girl into bed was to marry her.' He smiled, 'Mind, my father was very open and said, "The hungry have to be fed, so if you're not in bed by midnight, son, come home."'

It has to be said that young men were really quite honourable if a pregnancy was confirmed outside marriage. They knew that a young girl would suffer and remain a social outcast if she did not get a wedding ring on her finger pretty fast. Girls were much more ignorant where sex was concerned. The same gentleman said, 'We used to sow our wild oats and pray for a crop failure, if you know what I mean by that!'

I must admit I spoke to many who had experienced a shotgun wedding and most had gone on from strength to strength. Perhaps it was the way the young man had stood up to his duty, when a special respect was formed by the young girl who would otherwise have been in for a very tough time. Up until around the mid 1940s such women would have been forced to give up their baby for adoption; a heart-breaking time, the pain of which lingered for years.

Just to reinforce with what importance marriage was seen by

women I asked a very intelligent lady in her late seventies what sort of a career she would have followed had she been a young lady today. She looked at me in something akin to pity. 'I had a career, my dear, the best. I loved and was loved in return and raised three lovely, healthy children.'

So how did marriages of yesteryear thrive? Unless Daddy was reasonably wealthy and could offer the couple a home, or the bridegroom happened to work on a farming estate where cottages were generally made available, rent-free, upon marriage, most couples had to make do with compromise. And that meant starting off married life with one or the other set of parents.

Mrs Burton of Homersfield in Suffolk started off this way. 'My fiance and I were desperate to get married, in 1932. Quite simply, our bodies ached for the union of marriage. We had been courting

Caring for the home and family was a life's work for many women – here presiding over afternoon tea at The Elms, Old Catton.

for seven years, since I was 14. Marriage was the only sensible solution to our problem. I talked to my parents, who had the necessary knowledge, and they offered us a small front room and a bedroom. It worked very well, because apart from meal times when we all ate together, we kept ourselves to ourselves. Some of our friends thought we might suffer from jangled nerves due to the fact it was quite a small house and our bedroom was next to my parents'. This was a small disturbance since we had solved the real problem by marrying. After about three years we managed to save up a deposit for a home of our own. We had a very happy marriage and three children. I couldn't have asked for anything better.'

Of course, many marriages went 'off the rails', when one or other of the partners would have an indiscretion, but it seems this was no excuse for a divorce. 'Why rock the marital boat – marriage was never going to be plain sailing' was the general feeling. One gentleman, now in his early eighties and who wishes to remain anonymous for obvious reasons, put me in the picture. 'I was no saint. I cheated on my wife a few times when I was in my thirties. Perhaps it's because we had four kids and she was always tired and complaining of headaches. I was weak where other women were concerned. I didn't want to break up my marriage, just have a little fun, I suppose. Anyway, I did get one of my lady friends in the family way. She was married. Evidently her husband was of the same opinion as me and didn't want to break up the marriage either, so she had the baby and he brought it up as his own. The kid was none the wiser.' All very civilised and sensible, if it worked for both sides.

What did magazines advise prospective brides? *Woman* magazine 1954 had this advice on offer. 'Looking Lovely – Always' was the title: 'Your new life will include housekeeping, perhaps a job, entertaining, social life and – last but not least – lovely quiet evenings at home with your husband. Quite a tall order, especially if you take an effort to look your best – always.

'This "always" is one of the greatest differences between being a bachelor girl and a young wife. The bachelor girl, however busy,

Cosy Sitting-Room For £15

A Suggestion for the Woman Who Works and Wants a Friendly Background to Go Home to

(Furniture by Messrs Shoolbreds.)

A LITTLE typist in our office provided the inspiration.

"Moving *again?*" we said. "What a bother it must be always finding fresh apartments. Why don't you make a little home of your own?"

"There's nothing I should love more," she told us. "But furnishing is so expensive. If one could plan a sitting-room for something like fifteen pounds I should look around for rooms at once."

It seemed so sad to think of the number of women who must be living without any sort of friendly background because getting a home together appears such a costly proceeding.

There and then we decided to put on our thinking caps and in WOMAN AND HOME show what *could* be done if you have only a little to spend.

As a result we arranged the little living-room in our photograph.

ISN'T it a homey little place, and doesn't it seem wonderful to realise that anyone could have one like it for fifteen pounds?

It is all new furniture, and it is all well made.

WE began with the table—a gate-leg would suit our needs. These are pretty to look at and the ends fold down so conveniently, when you want more space.

Could you ask for anything more decorative?

The wheelback chairs, too, would grace any home; our sitting-room boasts two, one with arms and a slightly smaller chair without arms. They are both reproductions of the genuine old wheelbacks for which connoisseurs are ever scouring the countryside. Certainly there can be no question of the artistic merits of these chairs.

How the Fifteen Pounds is Spent

	£	s.	d.
Gate-leg Table	2	10	0
Wheel-back Chair	0	11	0
Wheel-back Arm-chair	1	5	0
Adjustable Easy Chair (with foot rest)	1	17	6
Adjustable Easy Chair	1	7	6
China Cabinet	4	15	0
Hair Carpet, 9 ft. by 7 ft. 6 in.	2	11	0

above and useful cupboard below.

With some decorative candlesticks up above, or a bowl of flowers, this cabinet is of great furnishing value. Perhaps it is hidden a little in our photograph.

We found the very thing for the floor in a cord carpet 9 ft. by 7 ft. 6 in. (You can obtain this in a variety of colours.) It will not entirely cover one's floor space—but then a surround of stained boards is always nice and much more convenient for keeping a room clean.

Oddments such as cushions, table runners and flower-bowls most women already possess. So we did not include them in our inventory. Such trifles cannot be standardised. Only your own little things will give the right personality.

If I were a business woman living alone I wouldn't stay in cheerless uncomfortable "diggings" one day longer. I'd begin saving up for a home of my own and I'd begin with a sitting-room like this, and shouldn't I be proud when friends dropped in to see me!

Armchairs, too, are important. On blustery days and when rain is chill a busy worker likes to think of cosiness and comfort waiting at "home."

The adjustable chairs we chose "go" splendidly with the scheme of the room and you will find nothing to beat them for ease.

One has a luxurious pull-out that makes it every bit as restful as a sofa. Both have backs which can be adjusted to suit your mood, and cosy mattress cushions.

ARE you wondering where you would room necessities? That is the rôle of the cabinet with its glass doors can make sure of looking her best when she meets her boyfriend; quick change and fresh make-up before letting him set eyes on her. When he's not around, there's no reason why she shouldn't slip on a baggy skirt and brother's discarded shirt and let her hair down (or pin it up) without caring two hoots about her looks.

'But that's exactly what a young wife can't do! It's a very silly outdated idea that once a girl is married she can wear any old thing at home, and keep her glamorous side for outings.

'After all, your husband chose you because he liked the way you looked, because he was proud of your taste, your choice of colour and style, your charm.

'In brief, he liked what he saw when he looked at you, and knew that he would not mind seeing it for the rest of his life. Isn't it only fair to stay the way he likes you to be?

'To look smart and pretty every night when he returns from work will be more of an effort than to put on glamour for your regular outings during your engagement. But seeing his eyes light up when he finds you in the kitchen, preparing a meal and looking attractive, will be a greater compliment than his compliment on a special date in your courting days. It's the little things that count.

'Your trousseau housecoat must be a smart affair. And to maintain its good looks it will have to be washed and crispened at least two days before it begs for a sound tubbing. Your bedroom slippers must not fall into a sad state of dejection, either.'

Now, all this briefing may seem crazy and modern women may raise a few laughs but marriage then was more than a fashionable institution. It was a way of life, for the rest of your life, and if a girl wanted her marriage to prosper, this sort of advice was felt to be important. If a husband came home, day after day, to a less than enthusiastic wife, and a dirty home, after a hard day's work, who would blame him for looking elsewhere?

Young men demanded a lot from their brides-to-be. Virginity was the magical state expected. As one gentleman said, 'If others had been there before you, you were not getting anything special, were you?' Having said that, young men stood up vigorously for their young ladies. If another fellow had his eyes on her he could expect a fight, or at the very least a severe ticking off.

To give some indication of how crucially affected the young men were by nice girls, listen to what Mr Bird of Hunstanton had to say. 'When I was a young lad growing up after the First World War, women were something of a mystery. Magical creatures with bright red lips who expected you to read their minds. With their hair fluffed up and eyes smiling, they left us young men in a bewitched state, I can tell you. If you got your legs under the table at her home, you were laughing. It meant she was serious about you.'

Honeymoons were just as nerve racking for the young men too. One gentleman, now in his seventies, muses, 'I was no pin-up myself and considered myself lucky when my girl agreed to marry me. Neither of us had any experience; on the honeymoon night it was a case of the blind leading the blind. I still don't know how I managed it although my mates had given me instruction.'

Marrying out of your class had dire consequences. Eddie Hemmant writes about a family he knew. 'Mildred was the very spoilt young daughter of a very rich elderly man. They lived in north Norfolk. Brought up in luxury, she had lovely clothes; everything she could possibly wish for. Her father idolised her and said she was fit to be a princess. He had great expectations for her.

'There were many young gardeners employed at the hall – amongst them was one Ruben. Ruben was good looking with black curly hair and blue eyes. Mildred often stopped to talk to him. Soon the head gardener noticed and gave Ruben a word of warning, "Don't talk so much with Miss Mildred, boy, or you may get dismissed." After this Ruben tried to avoid her but she had fallen in love and always found out where he was working. At last Ruben told her he was also in love, but he was a poor man and it would not do. He offered to leave the village and seek employment elsewhere – Mildred would not hear of it. She insisted they marry, saying her father would not let them want, she had always had everything she wanted.

In villages like Cley-next-the-Sea, girls would often marry the 'boy next door', or at least a local lad.

'They ran away and married in London. Mildred wrote to her parents and confessed. Her father was very angry and refused to answer her letters. Ruben was dismissed without a character reference. They returned to his parents' house but could not stay long in case his father got dismissed and lost the family home. Ruben found a labourer's job in another part of Norfolk; they lived in a small cottage on a small wage. Mildred had to do all her own housework and cook, something she had never in her life done before. They had one little daughter. Mildred never mixed with the village women and became quite reserved and lonely. She was a broken-hearted woman because her parents never forgave her and she never saw them again. Poor Mildred fretted herself into an early grave.'

Marrying within one's own class was the best chance one had

for happiness. In the early part of this century such rules were strictly observed. Marrying out of one's class was enough to turn one's mother's hair white overnight! It was that important.

All marriages were not made in heaven or created out of love. Convenience and respect played a big part in choice. Much more emphasis was placed on character and job prospects. Down to earth little creatures often married the boy next door, or one who at least lived in the village. The more adventurous lasses inspected the boys with a critical eye; they were not going to waste their glamour and talent on just anybody. These sort of girls could charm birds off trees and twist young men around their little fin-ger. Mrs Mayhew of Blundeston had one such sister who during

the Second World War 'held out' for an RAF officer she fancied. 'Trouble with my sister was she had become disillusioned with our fish and chip type of existence and dreamt instead of a champagne and caviare one.' Mrs Mayhew explains this sister caught her man and lived happily ever after in her new found higher lifestyle.

Mrs Simonds from Bury St Edmunds readily admits she was not in love when she married her husband in the 1930s. 'I had known him since schooldays. I was a dreadfully shy girl and never went out with anyone till we started courting, by chance really. He asked me to dance at a village hop and it went from there. My heart definitely did not go "bump, bump". The family liked him because he was clean, well-mannered and held a good job. We liked each other well enough but it was all one-sided. We sort of trailed into marriage but my love for him grew quickly after that because he was a tender man. Our love grew through a great understanding of each other's needs, mutual tenderness and consideration. He handed over his weekly pay packet; I gave him back enough for his weekly visit to the pub. He left the complete running of the home and finances to me. I never got us into debt although we were not what you would call well-off, especially when the three children came along.' Such marriages, founded on mutual consideration, often grew into great love affairs.

Mr Springall of King's Lynn remembers when he was seriously courting his young lady in the 1950s. 'Grandfather lived with us at the time. I worked on a farm and we only had a bath once a week, a tin bath in front of the fire. Well, I had my bath, shaved and was putting on some Old Spice to spruce up my natural smell. Grandfather asked what I was doing. I told him I had been sweating all day and was taking out my girl that night. He said, "In my young days a young lady would have given a man who used that stuff a wide berth." I retaliated, "You mean she would have preferred sweat?" He answered, "Yep! How else would she know who she had got hold on in the dark. With that pong she could a' bin kissin' anybody!"'

A few months after any marriage, news, which did not altogether surprise, reached the family. A baby was due. The marriage was well cemented – every female member started to knit.

It was after all, absolutely, what marriage was intended for.

Getting A Job

'I had half a day off once a fortnight on a Friday when I cycled the twenty miles home to enjoy tea with my own family.'

'What do you want to do when you grow up?' A timeless question put to many young children. As if there was much choice a few decades ago!

Answers, however, were varied and quite amusing; pretty romantic mental scenes and fancies were often stocked in the reply. 'I want to be a train driver,' was a popular reply with young boys, with 'I want to be a teacher,' a popular response from young girls. Occasionally a polite but clear little voice would pop an answer of a dream-like quality, 'I would like to be an army officer.' Short of a miracle or a military background, the chances of fulfilling such a wish were negligible. Children were allowed to dream on, because real life would catch them up soon enough.

However, most young people were realists – they had been taught by example. Their way forward was quite predictable. They were going out into the big wide world in search of any job that would bring in money. They had been conditioned from an early age – the harder you worked, the more money you brought home. Families needed money to survive. They were under no illusion, there just was no other way; unless, of course, Father came up on the pools, which was highly unlikely.

It must be observed that at the beginning of this century the population did not move about much. It was nothing unusual to spend the whole of one's life, from beginning to end, in one village. Every now and then one member of the family would go off in search of a fortune, and come back many years later with swanky clothes advertising his success. This person was always solemnly reminded about his roots. You see, those at home were perfectly preserved and hardened against outside forces – they didn't trust what they couldn't see.

Businessmen's sons, more often than not, followed in their father's footsteps. It was a foregone conclusion, whether that child had an interest or not. Working people had roots too, firmly implanted in the East Anglian soil and tradition. Country estates were owned by the aristocracy – whole families lived and worked on these very large properties extending to hundreds of acres. Whilst the men worked the land and livestock, both men and women secured domestic jobs in the big country house. These positions were many – maids, servants, domestic staff, nannies, butler, companions and cooks inside the house; whilst outside there were gardeners, grooms, nurserymen, stable boys, coachmen. It was nothing for a very large country house to employ anything up to 30 staff, in the house and gardens alone.

The owners of these large estates often treated their workforce quite fairly, simply because everybody relied upon everyone else. These big estates were rather like one huge family. There was an unwritten etiquette of ceremony which held the estate together. If, for example, a workman became ill, then the lady of the big house would make sure that his family did not suffer too dreadfully. Food would be taken to the cottage; an eye kept on their progress.

On one Norfolk estate, in a custom probably followed by others, the lady of the big house would provide a layette for every new baby born on the estate. This umbrella of security went further on the best estates, into retirement in fact. The retired were allowed to live in their cottage, providing they had spent their working life on the estate, rent-free till death.

'God helps those who help themselves' was drummed into

Phil Colman in 1927 – aged 14 and on his first Fordson tractor.

young heads from a very early age. Working was second nature to everyone, except those born with a silver spoon in their mouth!

Agriculture was the biggest employer. The tied-cottage system was a comfortable convenience, and if a farmworker were lucky in their choice of employer, they would get the odd tree-stump thrown in for fuel. Phil Colman of Old Catton left school to work on the family farm, but there   the good fortune ended. 'I left school at 14. Father bought me a secondhand tractor for £40 to keep me on the family farm. Times were bad and he couldn't pay me a wage. He suggested we rear some sow pigs and I could keep half the money we got from the offspring. A year later the sow was farrowing; I was over the moon. In the morning I went to feed her and to see how many pigs I had to sell. The sow was there – not one pig in sight, she had eaten them all. I had worked a year for nothing.'

The pace of life in the countryside was slow, with an ease which belied the heavy physical work. 'Mechanisation' was down to muscle power and real horse-power. The horses were like part of the family – loved and cared for, they had individual characters and were well versed in the work they had to do. Many of these horses did not have to be told, they knew what was expected.

Mr E. W. Firman of Ingham, Norfolk, spent 30 years as a cow-man. Like many, he has seen more changes in agriculture than anyone will see in the next 30 years. 'I left school on the first Monday in August 1942. I started work on a farm and was 14 three weeks later. This was before they changed August Bank Holiday to the end of the month. I milked cows by hand with my father on a smallholding. The cows were milked once a week by a 1½ horse-power engine as the petrol was rationed. We only had paraffin lanterns to see to milk and these cast weird shadows – we had to be

The 'little grey Fergie' TE20, which provided many farmers with their first experience of mechanised farming. (Massey Ferguson)

careful because the cows would lash out and kick, which was not very gentle. The linseed cake feed came in blocks and had to be ground by hand through the cake cutter; also the cattle beet and swedes had to be ground up with a hand cutter. The kale and chaff was done by machine in the barn.

'The farmer reared turkeys for Christmas – when they were young the farmer's wife would cut fresh nettle leaves, chop them up small and mix with bran mash for them, adding a bit of water. The hens laid about the buildings as they were allowed to run where they liked – the yolks were the colour of sunset.

'The milk was put in churns weighing 32 lbs empty, and held ten gallons, which was another 100 lbs. Each churn was labelled with the amount and the farmer's name. It was taken to the roadside for collection. Each man milked 16 cows twice a day. The calves were fed on their mother's milk for the first four days to give them a good start.

'At harvest time my father scythed round the edges of fields before the binder came and cut the corn.'

A lot of work on the farm was 'piece work', which meant workers got paid by the amount they did. Sugar beet, mangolds and turnips were all chopped out by hand hoe and the wage paid by this means. Those who worked fast obviously received more payment.

My own father worked his entire life on farms, caring for his cattle as if they were people. We either lived on or around farms and so we children became involved in little ways. As a twelve year old I used to go round up the cattle off the meadows, ushering them back for afternoon milking. One day 'Eileen', a good milker, took a dislike to me. Her tail went high and she bellowed; the next minute I was running with her in hot pursuit. My father and the head cowman Jack Frost were waiting at the edge of the field for me and the herd. Jack called for me to go over to them. I was in too much of a hurry and rushed past to the field gate, which I hurdled in seconds. Apparently I would have given Roger Bannister a run for his money that day!

My father loved his work and was always whistling. My sisters and I often used to watch him milk. One day he was hand milking, his head in the cow's side to facilitate hand movement. As we stood watching he tweaked an udder nipple in our direction, squirting milk into our faces. Of course, we found this a lot of fun. But then people laughed as they worked, years ago.

Phil Colman relates: 'I remember at Hill Farm, Roughton in the 1930s we had a harvest frolic when everything was gathered in. The neighbouring farmers were invited. We cleaned out the barn, put up trestles and a plank for a table, and forms to sit on. Mother played the piano, George on drum and me on the violin. Frank the head cowman sang *Among my souvenirs* in the broadest Norfolk accent. Mother's maid and the cook were spreading jam on bread and butter, the butler was filling up the men's beer glasses. One chap tried to stand up after 15 glasses and fell over, we put him in the car trailer and drove him home where two men put him in his shed to sober up. When it was dark things got going; dancing and singing. The girl cook danced with the young men. I noticed she was very kindly taking some of them outside for some "fresh air"! Father called it "Further Education"!'

Some girls just couldn't find the right job. Take Mrs Eileen Earl of East Winch, King's Lynn. What a gal she turned out to be. 'In 1941 I left school and got a job at the Co-op brush factory in Wymondham, Norfolk. I didn't like it much. I had to cycle twelve miles along a very lonely road in all weathers for ten shillings and sixpence a week. After one year I got the sack because I used to laugh too much with all the girls. When I got home on Friday with a week's notice in my pay packet, my parents were none too pleased.

'I thought I was going to have a little holiday – my dad had other plans. He told me to be up at six o'clock the next morning because there was a job going on the farm hoeing sugar beet. I then went on to milking and making butter, hay and straw casting and feeding pigs, bullock feeding and mangold grinding. One day the farmer told me to go and get a load of mangolds. Well, I got half a load. When I returned he said, "You don't call that a load, do you?" I told him I had got fed up. Once he sent me into a huge

John Chubbock (left) and two other farmworkers from Langley and Hardley, taking milk churns to Buckingham Ferry rail station.

field of fresh cut barley, it was all in shoves and had to be shocked up. Well, I stood a few up and then the barley haines got on my clothes so I went home to wash. Next morning he said, "You didn't do much in that field." I told him I was itching all over and very hot that day. I enjoyed those days but got married after four years, had four children and ended up being a gamekeeper and a housewife.'

John Fox is a cattle dealer who lives at Shipmeadow near Beccles. Dealing in cattle is in his blood. His father was Harry Fox, of Framingham Pigot near Norwich, who regularly attended the weekly cattle market sale in Norwich during the 1940s and 1950s. This weekly sale did brisk trade on Saturdays and was a meeting place for all those involved in farming. Most farmers and farmworkers, probably now retired, will have a tale to tell. Harry Fox dealt in Irish cattle. He was paid five shillings a head commission; a lot of money in those days,

The drovers were paid handsomely too. There were a half dozen regular drovers who drove the cattle to market from grazing land adjacent to the old Pineapple Hotel in Trowse. These cattle had travelled by train to Norwich Thorpe Station and had been grazed either one or two nights in readiness for the trek up Bracondale and down Ber Street to the market. Other men would be waiting at the Pineapple, in the hope of being able to help and earn. A drover could expect to receive ten shillings for one day's work. The owners of the grazing land in Trowse charged one shilling per head per night.

The reader can guess what sort of mayhem ensued as the cattle walked, and sometimes ran, along the busy streets of Norwich. Shoppers ran into any shop available when unruly cattle passed.

My own father often walked a bull or two from Caister St Edmunds where he worked as a cowman. 'I usually had another man with me to stand in gateways and roadways. We started off very early in the morning. When we passed greengrocery shops, the shopkeepers would come out and guard their produce otherwise the stuff would have disappeared.'

Earlier this century women were bundled off into domestic service if the family could not afford to keep them at home. Some fortunate women who were nimble with the thimble earned a living in the dressmaking trade, but for the majority a domestic existence beckoned.

Mrs Kathleen Dearg of Sea Palling is 72. At 14 she was sent to work in a big farmhouse at Ormesby near Great Yarmouth. She was not at all happy with her occupation: 'I used to cycle from Hickling. I had to cook for two but many times for a family of seven. At least we had a lady to scrub the floors. I did the bedrooms and housework. I had a half day off on Wednesday and another on Sunday. A nasty moment I'll never forget, was coming down the stairs and seeing smoke coming from the oven. My meat pie was black. I had to quickly think for myself because there was no one to ask. I cut off the burnt, made some more pastry and baked again, watching it this time. As we had lovely farm butter, I

Norwich cattle market in the late 1940s. The Castle Mall stands on this site today. (Eastern Counties Newspapers)

had to make home-made bread; it was no use saying "can't". My mother hated sending me out to work but couldn't afford to keep me at home.

'On my half days I cycled home and had to be back in at 10 pm and report to the mistress. Mum used to cycle some of the way back with me. I got half a crown a week and out of that I had to buy a pair of stockings each week for one shilling. I had to wear a blue dress and white apron in the mornings; brown dress and coffee coloured apron and cap in the afternoons. I still dream about not having a clean white apron – it was so important.

'After a while I left as Mum thought the work was all too much for me. I was 15 by then and went to another big house near Ormesby church to work with my sister. I wasn't at all happy because she made me do all the nasty jobs; vegetables, washing up and washing floors. Night times were terrible; we slept in the loft. We had a ladder for stairs which we had to pull down; it was worse when we had to come down. Our mistress was an invalid, elderly and very strict.

'When war broke out I came nearer home, once again to a farmhouse. This house was in Hickling near the Broads. I was able to live at home and go there daily which was great but, alas, I had to stay for tea. I only had bread and butter, no cakes. The mistress used to count them to see if I'd taken any. I used to put mustard on my bread and butter for flavour because I wasn't allowed jam.'

This was a pattern of employment which many experienced. Minding your Ps and Qs was what it was all about. In other words, showing utter loyalty and respect for those you worked for, no matter what you felt. Settling in was always painful because the young girls were barely in their teens when they left home to work. Homesickness was very real. The hearts of mothers must have ached till they almost broke but they were obliged to send their daughters out to work.

Life was harsh for the young people, although most soon recovered from their unhappy state, especially when they became friendly with other members of staff. Relationships developed, of course, between young indoor female and young outdoor male staff, which must have made life a whole lot sweeter. However, meeting behind the mulberry bush had to be devilishly well planned, because time wasted in courting was not approved of by the mistress of the house. Concealing a courtship was all part of the exquisitely risqué business!

Joan Alden of Surlingham is 75 years young. When she left school in 1936 she was not quite sure what she wanted to do but felt she would like to work with children. She takes up her story: 'I decided to take a live-in situation which was being advertised for someone "fond of children". The house, on the Norfolk coast, was large and overlooked the sea, which was a new experience for me having lived all my life deep in the quiet wooded countryside. There were two children, a boy and a girl, with a baby on the way.

*A parlourmaid collecting the daily quota of milk for the house –
Northrepps Hall in 1900 – busily chatting to the yard-boy.*

'It was soon established that I would do some housework until I got to know the children better. My first job of the day was to clean the grates in the sitting room and dining room, then re-lay the fires. There were no Hoovers in those days; I had to get down on my hands and knees with brush and dustpan, then dust and polish. Then the front doorstep had to be scrubbed and the brass name plate by the gate had to be polished, even in very cold weather. I also had to clean all the family footwear, making sure the underneath was wiped clean as well. Meanwhile, Cook had started preparations for breakfast; I had to go upstairs and get the children out of bed, which they were often very reluctant to do, bathe and dress them, take them down to their mother and father waiting in the sitting room. It all appeared calm as I handed them over, but it had been a mad tussle to get them that far.

'By this time breakfast was ready and I had to wait table, which I had previously laid. From rising at 5.30 am till 8 am when everyone was sitting down to breakfast, I felt I'd done a day's work but it was far from over. Beds had to be made, floors had to be washed. Different days had one main job to be done. Monday was devoted to washing the household linen, but I was never allowed to hang it out. I often longed to walk in the garden or play with the children, but it was out of bounds to me.

'Tuesday was bathroom scrubbing day; bath, basin, tiled walls had to be cleaned. Fresh linen from the day before's wash had to be put in the cupboards.

'Wednesday was brass cleaning day. All the stair rods from three flights of stairs were taken out, polished and replaced. I had Wednesday afternoons off; I would walk along the shore and look in a few shops along the way. Wednesday was colloquially known as "skivvies' day" as all the girls who worked in the big houses and hotels had the same afternoon off. I got to know quite a few and made friends.

'I hated the day when the larder and pantry had to be cleaned out. There was masses of crockery to be washed, shelves and floors to be scrubbed and the crockery to be put back. Sometimes there were guests for dinner.

'I had half a day off once a fortnight on a Friday when I cycled the twenty miles home to enjoy tea with my own family. Our cottage seemed like a little nutshell after the large rooms of the house where I worked. I told Mother that in the early days of my working life I would often find a half-crown coin tucked down the side of an armchair or even under a rug. Mother explained it was a ploy to test the honesty of the servants. The coins were placed deliberately and had I kept any of them, I would have been questioned and sacked. I remember feeling very hurt that I had not been trusted.

'I continued there for another year, always with the hope that I would eventually look after and play with the children, but I never did. I did housework, all for 7s 6d a week. I left, came home and went to work in a shop in Norwich.'

Mrs Alden's story is typical of the long hours put in by those in service. The big households expected their staff to keep up a certain standard of cleanliness. In fact, mistresses were often ruled by an obsession to keep everything spotlessly clean. Cleanliness played no small part in overcrowded and smaller households, either. It was the proper way to look after the family. Hot water systems were not so civilised as today and so jug and basin sets in the bedroom were filled by a servant carrying up hot water in a brass pouring can.

It must also be remembered that furniture and furnishings were handed down the generations; it was the duty of the mistress of the house to see that all was well looked after, so there was a very good reason for all the toil.

Contracts of employment were thin on the ground; usually quite simply, they did not exist. Getting a job was so important to some that they started work without knowing what sort of wage would be coming their way at the end of the week. Mr C. J. Nicholls of Loddon was very disappointed after his first week. 'I left school at the start of the Second World War. I was promised a job at Langley Hall, the residence of Lord and Lady Beauchamp. Unfortunately the army moved into the hall and took over the

The cook and kitchenmaid at the rectory where Amy Glenister worked, 1928.

grounds. This was Christmas 1940 – no work was forthcoming until the following April. I cycled five miles to Hardley from Claxton to work on a market garden. I worked from Monday to Saturday lunchtime. Eager to draw my first week's pay, my employer asked me how much I wanted. I replied 15 shillings and eightpence halfpenny. He told me he could not afford that, he thought I would require about ten shillings. So that was the start and finish of my first week's employment. I cycled home a very unhappy boy. I am 70 now and still remember that day.'

Vicars employed staff in years gone by. Many of them lived in quite large rectories, and were respected on a par with others in authority. Mrs Amy Glenister of Brandon is 'getting on in years' but vividly remembers her job at the rectory: 'I left school at 14 to help in the rectory nursery. There were four indoor staff; a cook, kitchenmaid, parlourmaid and housemaid. I never really wanted to be a nursery-nurse but because my mother had been a children's nurse she decided I should be one too. We did as we were told in those days. The nursery meals were sent up from the kitchen; there was a night nursery and a day nursery, both of which I had to keep clean and tidy. I was quite happy there until my mother became ill. I had to return home to help as my parents kept the village public house.' Mrs Glenister finished by saying, 'If I was young again and could go back to those days, I would go.'

Housekeepers could be less than friendly, as Mrs Dawson of Norwich recalls. 'There were six of us under a housekeeper. She was a tyrant, and really quite uninterested in any good we did. Even the master of the house was in fear of her. He only dared smile faintly at us when she was around; at other times he was very cheerful and talkative. Some of us domestics worked "like stink" for sometimes little praise.'

Farming families automatically put their daughters to work at home. Even if the pay was small, their daughters were out of harm's way at home and, best of all, able to sleep in their own bed at night. The many obstacles of working away left these young ladies in no doubt about their good fortune. However, this life

Violet Everett, Amy Glenister's friend in service, 1927.

could be very restricting and many of these young girls stayed single for much longer, simply because they did not meet many eligible young men.

Many were so shielded from outside influences that they did not marry at all. As one lovely lady in her late seventies declares: 'I never did marry because every young man who looked my way, Mother sent packing. Nobody was ever good enough for me as far as she was concerned. I got so fed up with Mother's attitude at times but could do nothing about it short of leaving home and I had nowhere to go and very little money to my name because I did not actually receive a wage. When I needed new clothes, Mother bought them for me.'

There was more choice for those living in built up areas. The railways, for example, offered a good career. Mr W. N. Ladbrooke of Gorleston on Sea started work on the L&NE Railway in 1935 at the age of 14. 'My job was to run in front of the train with a red flag to stop the traffic and an iron bar to change the points to whichever way the shunter wanted the train to go. The work was very tiring. When the fishing season started things got very hectic; I had to run from Vauxhall station to the Fishwharf two or three times daily. The first week of the herring season we went on two shifts, 6 am to 2 pm and 2 pm to 10 pm. This was a very busy period, bringing coal to the fishing boats and taking fish products back to the station, besides dealing with timber and fertilizer ships

A Lowestoft smack.

that unloaded on the rivers. I once worked two shifts because the relief man did not turn up. I was so tired I fell asleep whilst holding the points lever and it slipped out of my hand, so the points closed and half the train was on the line and the other half was on another. I got into a hot bath when I got home and fell asleep; I didn't wake up until the water was cold!'

Every young person fully expected to start at the bottom and climb the promotional ladder in due course. They knew those at the top had started in the same way. Many stayed in one job for all their working life and received a gold watch upon retirement.

Some young people were like knicker elastic, they liked to stretch their talents. Peter Sayers of Stockton near Beccles left school in 1940 at 14 years of age. His family had moved from Norwich and his Norfolk exam results were worthless 'over the border'. 'I was denied a grammar school education, so from the secondary modern I started work at Read Owles & Ashford, Auctioneers and Estate Agents – a job my father found for me, following in Grandad's footsteps. A few months of sales ledger balancing proved too much and so I moved up into Hungate to William Robinson, Motor and General Engineers. This was not a good career move; changing a suit for overalls at two shillings a week less.

'However, by the time I was 16 I could carry out virtually any work needed to repair any sort of vehicle; be it bike, car, truck or tractor. Most skilled mechanics were in the forces by then. A £5 loan from Mother secured my first motor bike at 15 and I was legally on the road at 16, by then as an essential worker. Thanks to the Home Guard I could drive by the age of 18, rebuild vehicles and shoot straight, which held me in good stead because I was called up into the Army at 18.'

Peter's wife, Iris, worked her way up the ladder at Messrs Clowes printing works in Beccles. 'In August 1945 I became a very junior member of the counting house staff. I continued in this department for three years, gradually progressing from post girl at a wage of 2s 6d to a more interesting clerical position with a suitable wage increase to 7s 6d. My real interest was in books, so

A Norfolk wherry transporting goods inland.

when a chance came for me to go into the bindery department, I took the plunge. Here I learnt how to cost out materials used in the production of the books. I also had many opportunities to witness things like hand tooling and gold blocking which I enjoyed, and found myself there up until my marriage in 1953.'

Towards the end of the Second World War opportunities were presenting themselves, although young people had to prove themselves capable and efficient. Office work was all hand-work and so a neat hand was essential. A good command of English grammar and punctuation was expected too.

Relationships with employers were respectful and guarded. It would have been quite rude to call a director, or an elderly employer, by their Christian name. Accordingly they held the same respect for their staff and always referred to them by title, as Miss So-and-So or Mrs So-and-So. This sort of dignity was second nature to all. Even a good telling off was done politely.

After the war secretarial jobs became popular for young women. Typewriting and shorthand courses were offered to those who could afford the fees. Young ladies were taught to not only type correctly, but dress in a businesslike manner, sit in a certain way when taking dictation, and to remain professional at all times. This teaching extended to speech. To this day most ex-secretaries have what is commonly known as a telephone voice.

Most ordinary families did not have telephones and the Post Office employed telegram boys for urgent messages. Richard Michael Fisk of Reydon near Southwold in Suffolk has written a small book for his family about his postal career during the years 1947 to 1992 and recalls: 'I was still at school when a family friend, George Gerrell, called at our home one evening to ask if I'd like to join the Post Office as a messenger boy. George was already employed at Southwold post office. I jumped at the chance and attended after school and on Saturdays. One of the questions on my application form asked, "Can you ride a bike?" I was a tall lad which was just as well because every bicycle was a sit-up-and-beg model. I left school at 14 and started full time.

'I was one of two messengers, otherwise known as telegram boys. We had to wear a uniform of thick blue jacket and trousers and waistcoat, and a pillarbox hat with red piping; the hat badge was brass and had to be regularly cleaned. We wore a thick leather belt which had an attached oblong pouch for our telegrams, and for forms should anyone want to send a reply. We never knew the contents of the telegram although the clerk did warn us if the news was not good. We were then prepared for a reaction. Whilst waiting for telegrams we spent our time unravelling pieces of string which came from bundles of inward letters.'

During the war women's lives were transformed dramatically. There was a shortage of manpower in all sorts of jobs because the men were sent off to war. Women who had previously failed to produce anything more commercial than washing and ironing were suddenly offered employment in munition factories. They also descended onto the land in great numbers; the Land Army girls brought a little more than effort with them, they brought glamour into the fields.

Working outside in the open appealed to a lot of women, so much so that after the war they were reluctant to go back to just plain domestic chores. I remember my own dear mother working on the land in the early 1950s. Father worked for James Cargill at Norton Hall, as a cowman. Mr Cargill also grew vegetables. A variety of jobs were on offer for local women – stringing the beans, potato riddling, picking the beans when fit, picking soft fruits.

My sisters and I went along with Mother in the school holidays to help her pick. It was a lot of fun outside in the sunshine. Picking raspberries generally coincided with the school holidays, as did blackcurrant picking. I was fascinated by the small-talk which went on amongst the women. Innuendo was rife and I was old enough to read between the lines, so to speak. As the heads bobbed up and down so the talk flowed. Considerable conversation about family took place. Gossiping about others out of earshot was often at fever pitch too. Oh, how my mother loved her days in the fresh air, earning money for a little independence. Alas, mechanisation has denied local women these pleasures.

The world has changed dramatically in these last 50 years. I doubt we shall see such changes in the next 50 years. Who knows, perhaps the easy harmony of yesteryear will once again invade our lives and our work.

Keeping Healthy

'Many people take a vast interest in drugs and all the paraphernalia of a doctor's shop, who would be much better in seeing that their food was good in quality, well prepared and suitable to their constitutions' – Good Wife's Cook Book 1930.

A sk any older person how many times they visited the doctor as children, and the reply will astound. 'Hardly ever!'

Except for well-known killer diseases, or severe casualties, all nursing was done by Mother, at home. Whatever the condition the suggested road to recovery was the same; plenty of rest and quiet, supplemented by nourishing home-made food suitable for the convalescent.

For health was a serious business, for good reason. If the man of the house lost valuable days to illness, the family lost money. However, providing the man of the house was fit and capable of work, the family did not suffer – the main priorities being a roof over the head and food on the table. Expectations did not look far beyond these principles in the early part of this century. When I asked an aged gentleman, who had been one of 14 children in the early 1900s, about food scares, he laughed. 'Food scares! The only thing that scared us was the possibility of not having enough to eat at dinner time.'

Up until July 1948 when the National Health Service came into being, many families paid one penny per week to a nursing association to cover any nursing expense. Doctors were only called by the very rich. The poor had to make do, in worrying times, with

the district nurse. There were many societies which insured against illness; most families paid into one or the other.

Every household boasted a comprehensive First Aid tin and thermometer. As one 75-year-old smiled, 'I had more thermometers stuck into my mouth than sweets when I was a child. I only had to cough and Mother ordered a test.' Another lady recalls, 'We had weekly doses of syrup of figs to keep us regular, sulphur tablets in spring to clean the blood and a jar of Vick on constant standby for wheezy chests.'

'Smelling salts, too,' recalled another. 'My father always swore by these to clear up the most brutal of headaches.'

No woman's education was considered complete unless she had acquired some knowledge of home nursing. Much of this educating was done in the home through personal experience and wisdom handed down the generations.

All sorts of conditions prevailed years ago. Normal childhood ailments like chicken-pox, German measles, measles, mumps, whooping-cough and scarlet fever did the rounds and were treated by a vigilant, caring mother until the child was up and about again. However, the more serious conditions, such as diphtheria and bronchitis were subject to doctor's visits. In the worst cases, children were carried off to the isolation, or fever, hospital.

Good health was maintained by good home-cooked fresh food. In the country, all vegetables were grown in large back gardens, while those who did not have ample space rented allotments to keep the family well and truly nourished. Every housewife knew that the body resembled an engine. And like an engine it needed fuel. Food was fuel – they knew without it the body would suffer. Ask any very old person what their secret of longevity is and they will almost certainly attribute their great age to 'good food and plenty of it'.

Individual diets were recognised as being very important. Here's what the *Good Wife's Cook Book* of 1930 had to say: 'Many people take a vast interest in drugs and all the paraphernalia of a doctor's shop, who would be much better in seeing that their food was good in quality, well prepared and suitable to their constitutions. It

would be unwise, for example, to give an invalid roast pork, although to the strong digestion it is very nutritious, while to provide a working navvy with chicken broth would be rather to invite his contempt; when a good steak would secure his admiration.'

This is further strengthened by the comments of a 91-year-old gentleman. I asked him if he were on any special drugs. He looked

A breath of sea air for the author (right), her mother and sister Jennifer in 1950.

at me aghast. 'If folk paid more attention to what they ate, they wouldn't need them.' Suffice to say he was not on medication of any sort, turned over his garden regularly to bury the contents of his outside loo and walked straighter than many much younger men.

If a breadwinner became unfit for work, the first thing the neighbours did was ensure the family got enough to eat. They bent over backwards to this end by providing enough food for that family until the person in question was back to full working strength.

All sorts of extraordinary cures were handed down the generations, which seemed to work extremely successfully. Margaret Turner of Thurlton is 81 and remembers a very messy remedy for a bad chesty cold. 'Mother would spread goose grease on brown paper, place it upon the chest, put a piece of linen over the lot to keep it secure, until the complaint eased.'

I remember when growing up in the 1940s and 1950s a doctor's visit was rare. We used hot poultices for boils, dock leaves for stings, raw onions rubbed over wasp stings, and boiled horseradish for colds. Dad went even further in his endeavour to rid himself of a major cold. He boiled onions in milk. To my knowledge he never had a day off work as a herdsman. He, too, swore by smelling salts.

Being unwell carried a little joy, because there was no onus on getting well quickly. Slow recovery was then seen as being better than a fast recovery. The remedies had to have time to work, during which time the young patient was thoroughly spoiled. Extra books were read at the bedside, any misdoings were overlooked. In my experience, a little bout of something or other was quite enjoyable!

Transport – Cars, Cycles and Charabancs

━━━━ ❧ ━━━━

'When I was a child we didn't have holidays like people do today. We had an annual day out to the seaside in a coach or charabanc. We always finished up in Great Yarmouth. It was only twenty miles away from where we lived but for all we knew we could have been travelling the length of Britain.'

We will journey back into time to the turn of this century. Old Jimmy Smith of Harleston was enjoying a pint in the pub when somebody got on the piano. *Did you ever go across the sea to Ireland?*, the ivories tinkled out their melody. Old Jimmy knocked back the remains of his pint and laughed, 'I did once and got me feet wet. Nivver again…'

The whole place shook with laughter. Everyone present could just imagine old Jimmy in a strange country with his tatty suitcase in his hand looking for board and lodgings. You see, Jimmy was almost 60 years old and had only been out of Harleston twice in his life. Travel in those days was no more than a joke.

The pleasures of travel were only for the rich, or those unfortunate enough to have experienced war. Those who craved adventure just had to content their curiosity with a book. A Beccles man, now well in his eighties, remembers when he went to Bungay in his youth, with a couple of pals. 'We soon hotfooted it out of town because the local boys thought we were after their girls. We were foreigners to them and up to no good at all.'

Another East Anglian gentleman remembers when he left home

At Salhouse Broad Farm in the early 1900s.

in the 1920s. 'Mother was suffering from TB and couldn't look after me, so I was sent to stay with an aunt in London for a couple of months. When Mother's health improved I returned home…to a hero's welcome. I was treated like a celebrity and made to tell my tale over and over again. I felt like Dick Whittington!'

The population walked everywhere. Earlier this century people thought nothing of walking miles to and from work each day. Walking for its own sake was a national pastime in any case, especially on Sunday afternoons.

Mr Neave of Attleborough recalls: 'I remember an acquaintance who regularly, in summer, walked six or seven miles from Clare in Suffolk to Long Melford, just to spend Sunday with his son and family. Then back again in the evening. Then there was the preacher who lived in Lavenham. He walked to Melford each Sunday to take service in the Congregational church and then walked back again, a distance of ten miles!'

Wily country folk hitched rides on the top of farm carts which were going into town. It was nothing out of the ordinary to see people sitting, perhaps a little uncomfortably, on top of a cart full of potatoes or apples. It saved on shoe leather.

The wealthy travelled more comfortably. Such people kept a coachman whose main occupation was to see to the horses and upkeep of the family carriage. Those who owned such transport could make longer journeys and seek their everyday needs from shops further afield. The more successful businessman would keep a pony and trap in which he and his family could travel distances to visit friends and relatives.

When I was growing up in Dunston near Norwich in the late 1940s we lived next to a Mr and Mrs Holmes. This nice gentleman had a pony and trap, the sort that opened at the rear and was known as a governess cart. Each Sunday I would board this sweet little cart along with his own children and we would all be elegantly transported to Sunday school in Stoke Holy Cross village hall. I found it a bit tricky getting into the cart because it unnervingly plunged downwards when a person set foot on the little hanging-down step. The seats were lengthwise each side of the trap and so we passengers could see both front and rear of the road. It was a lovely way to travel and nothing since has ever equalled that Sunday pony and trap treat.

After the First World War transport improved considerably. Converted field ambulances ran people about. Local bus companies soon got on the bandwagon and ran services all over East Anglia, taking villagers into town two or three days a week.

An appetite for travelling was beginning and the motor car was making more of an appearance. Local dignitaries, doctors and the wealthy were driving themselves around. Doctors especially found this mode of transport to their liking since it meant they could get to their patients much more quickly than on horseback.

Charabancs became popular with an ever increasing number of working people. These vehicles carried them on outings to the seaside, rivalling the railway day excursions.

I remember these excursions well. When I was a child we didn't have holidays like people do today. We had an annual day out to

A horse and cart on the Wroxham Road, Norwich in August 1953.
(Eastern Counties Newspapers)

Mr and Mrs S. J. Watts of Upton, off for a drive in their donkey trap in December 1962. (Eastern Counties Newspapers)

the seaside in a coach, or charabanc. We always finished up in Great Yarmouth. It was only twenty miles away from where we lived but for all we knew we could have been travelling the length of Britain. The coach was filled up with beer, ginger beer, sandwiches and cakes and we were so excited. Everybody in that coach knew each other and it was a real spree. We were laughing from the moment we entered the coach till the moment we arrived. Once in Yarmouth we walked along the front with ice creams in our hands, had donkey rides on the beach, played with our spades and pails, and ate our sandwiches on the beach, which was a mistake really because the munching of grit was not at all pleasant, but we cared not. On the journey home, the grown ups broke into song. We talked about that day out for months after.

Cycles were a popular form of travel for those who could afford them. However, these required a certain amount of skill because the early cycles were very high; commonly known as 'highsteppers'. Women particularly found this difficult to master because fashion dictated long skirts. Mrs Field of North Walsham recalls: 'My father purchased me a highstepper in the early 1930s. I found the technique of pedalling and balancing very tedious. Father had to run alongside me at first, holding on to the saddle. I must confess to a feeling of inadequacy when I realised he had let go and left me on my own. I fell off many times before I learnt to ride that bike, but oh my goodness, it gave me such freedom.'

Of course a few scorch marks on the backside and a little gravel rash did not deter. Leaving behind the effort of walking is ably described by a gentleman from Wickham Market: ' When I got my first bicycle in 1928 I felt I was king of the road. Trouble was we lived down an unmade loke covered with rough and loose stones. There were plenty of hollows in that loke too and many was the time I flew over the top of my handlebars. Of course it traded me well for girls. I often picked up a stray and weary female and sat her on my crossbar.'

Phil Colman recalls a period when his family were farming at Hill Farm, Roughton in the 1930s. 'This young man was very proud of his new racing bike. He had saved about three years to get the £11 to buy it. He carried it over the mud in the farmyard, cleaned and polished it every day.

'Now, things went a bit wrong for him! His girlfriend told him, "We must get married, soon." Oh, dear! No money – only a bike. He tried to sell it to all the men he knew… £6, £5, £4 – he could not find a buyer; nobody had any money to spare. Wages at that time were around £1 10s a week. Time was getting short. One morning he came to me when I was loading milk onto my trailer. "Please give me £3 for the bike – I am b……. if you don't." Now, what could I do? He really made me feel sad. So I put the bike on my trailer and gave him £3. He said, "Thanks, you have saved me." My brother had just started a job as a barber in

Miss Hannah Rogers of Northrepps, on her round in 1940.

Cromer so I gave the bike to him as a birthday present.

'As the wedding day got near Father told the young man in question that he would drive him to the church and lend him £1. Ten bob to pay the parson and the rest for beer. The couple got bits of furniture from their relations – what a start to married life! Father never did get his £1 back.'

My own mother was a Norwich girl. At the age of 16 her mother brought her a cycle, a light-framed racing version. Mother and her friends cycled everywhere. 'After tea we would think nothing of cycling up to ten miles out into the countryside. At the weekends we cycled to Great Yarmouth or Cromer.'

When my father was growing up in Harleston, Norfolk, in the 1920s, he remembers a vehicle coming into the town each week. 'It was the only vehicle we saw and it was a dickie type. A couple of seats in front for the driver and his passenger with a back section which lifted to reveal two more seats for any extra passengers.' This vision of internal combustion excited the people of Harleston. It was not long before more and more motor cars appeared in the small towns.

Phil Colman remembers: 'My father had the first Model T Ford in the area in 1922. It was also a first in that it had black lamps. Previously the cars sported brass lamps and brass radiators. Before he bought that car Father travelled everywhere on horseback. The early car drivers looked like a cross between a driver and pilot because they wore those helmet-type hats very similar to flying helmets.'

In 1935, the driving test was introduced to a nation eager to own a car. This test was for new drivers and so those who had ruled the road before this date were excused and never had to pass a test. Like many of his generation, my father has never taken a test and, touch wood (done), had never had an accident in all his years of driving. Like many of his generation, too, he does not think much of modern day drivers, 'Mad blighters'!

However, learning to drive was not all honey. Maurice Winter of Gorleston recalls a driving incident sometime in the early

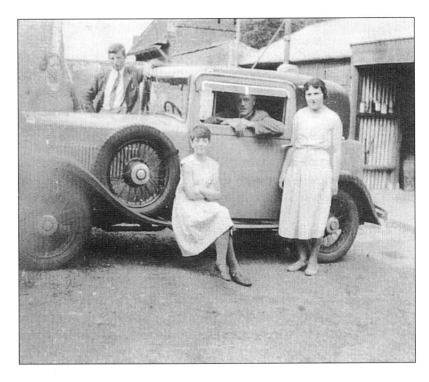

Georgina Manser's father and family at Loddon in 1933. She remembers the fun the family had with with this new form of transport.

1930s. 'Father purchased a brand new Austin 10. He had lessons but could not get the idea of straightening out after negotiating a corner. One day he drove round a corner and hit a tree. This put him off driving and he gave up, declaring he was too old.' His daughters learnt to drive. One, Hilda Constance, became a very good driver and kept it up for many years. Joyce, another daughter, was what one might call an enthusiastic driver.

'One day, she took May Alice, my mother, and myself out for a spin in the country. May Alice was in the front passenger seat, I was in the back. We passed through Wymondham, travelling down the A11 towards Attleborough; as we approached the handkerchief bends (these are long gone now) Joyce entered the bends much too fast and skidded right over to the offside of the road. Fortunately, nothing was coming in the opposite direction; if there had been we might have all been killed. Some young men in a following car overtook us and pretended to skid all over the road, taking the mickey out of us. They thought this was a bit of a lark but May Alice was not amused and reported it to George Henry. What the outcome was I don't know but I don't remember Joyce driving the car any more after that incident.'

When I was eleven, in 1953, my father secured another cowman's job, this time at Norton Hall near Reedham Ferry. We lived at Hill Cottages, Heckingham. We were a three-mile walk from the Eastern Counties bus route, although a bus did venture our way once a week. It went to Beccles, allowing people from local villages a two-hour shopping spree before setting back again. Father's new job meant he did three-times-a-day milking. He was up at the crack of dawn to milk, home for breakfast, back to feed the calves, home for lunch, when he usually managed a round or two of digging in the garden, back for the afternoon milking session. Home for tea then back to milk again. He usually got home about 9.30 pm. These long hours secured him a nice weekly pay packet.

One day off, Mum and Dad went to Norwich. They came home with a converted Austin 10 van; it had been converted so that the whole had windows very much like a regular car. Dad remembers the registration number, AAH 677. I must say I felt very proud. None of my friends' parents had cars, so this acquisition boosted my social standing no end.

When Dad had a day off we would all jump into this van and visit my grandmother at Stoke Holy Cross, or the other grandmother at Norwich. We nearly always stopped at a pub on the way home. Mum and Dad would go inside and bring out Vimto and crisps for we three girls sitting outside. We were a jovial family with quite a lot of friends. That little van was often bursting at the seams. Dad recalls, 'Very often I had to ask some of the passengers to get out so that the van could

Traffic outside the Poultry Mart, Norwich in 1936. (Eastern Counties Newspapers)

negotiate a hill. It was a bit sluggish at times.'

Gorleston on Sea wondered what had hit it one day when we arrived, complete with a neighbouring family. Dad takes up the story: 'When we got to Gorleston I parked in front of a small parade of shops. There were nine of us crammed into the van and when I opened the back doors you all started to scramble out. A shopkeeper came rushing out, waving her hands in the air, telling me we couldn't park there as we were blocking the view of her shop. I remember there were a couple of policemen over the road watching us in astonishment. We were like a Noah's ark on wheels. I said to the shopkeeper, "Don't yew fret, missus, there are hundreds more of them to get out as yet." As you all filed out, the policemen over the other side were roaring with laughter.'

A scene of heavy snowfall near Wroxham in 1952. (Eastern Counties Newspapers)

How did the police themselves fare as far as travel went? Remember, please, that the population, as a whole, were very respectful to those who upheld law and order in the community. Local on-the-beat bobbies were feared by the youngsters because they knew if they got out of order they could expect a ding of the ear from the bobby and another from Father when they returned home.

In Norfolk in 1896, the Chief Constable sent for a bicycle from the manufacturers and attempted to persuade the Police Authority to purchase some. The request was refused; the Chief Constable was authorised to hire one in an emergency but the officer using it would do so at his own risk. In the main therefore, up until the early 1920s the method of transportation by the County Police

Supt Roy at East Dereham in 1920.

was on foot or horseback. In 1919 the Police Authority purchased nine Ford cars, presumably for use by the superintendents. Three motorcycles were also purchased for the use of chief inspectors who were responsible for larger sub-divisions, ie Acle, Loddon, Terrington. So far as can be established from archives, the Norfolk County Police, which existed as a separate force until 1968, never provided their officers with bicycles, but did give a cycle allowance to individual officers. It is probable that by the late 1920s most officers were taking advantage of this allowance and using their own bicycles.

By the late 1950s more and more of the general public were purchasing cars; Acts of Parliament regarding this mode of transport came into being. The ten-year MOT test was introduced in 1958. In 1968 as part of the motor vehicle construction, a law came in relating to tyre tread. Before that date some motorists were economising and running their vehicles on almost bald tyres.

Norfolk Constabulary with the new intake of motorcycles, outside Norwich Divisional Headquarters, Thorpe Road, 1931.

The Motor Patrol section of Norfolk County Police with their 18/85 Wolseleys in 1939.

Jimmy Saville, the well-known radio and TV personality, pro-
moted a new seat-belt law passed in 1983, in an endeavour to
promote safety on our busy and fast roads.

On 25th November 1896 the *Eastern Daily Press* carried a story.
It went like this: 'Yesterday, a public parade of the motor car, now
on exhibition at Bostock & Wombwells, took place through the
streets of Norwich allowing citizens to form an opinion on the
merits and demerits of the new style of locomotion. The proces-
sion was led by a band and took an extended route. At the market
place one spectator said it appeared as if an ordinary carriage had
run away down Guildhall Hill.'

A hundred years later, almost to the exact month, the *Eastern
Daily Press* carried a letter from one of its many readers. 'I write to
enquire whether someone with local knowledge would enlighten
me as to what crime the villagers of Long Stratton committed in
the past resulting in them being abandoned to the dangers of the
motor car.' This letter referred to a proposed bypass which had
been shelved by the Department of Transport.

How sad that this miracle of locomotion has turned into such a
monster.

Index